How To Make
Your Business
Run Without You!

Streamline Your Business Operations to Pave the Way for:
More Business, Bigger Profits
and a Business that Virtually Runs Itself!

Susan M. Carter

First Edition
Second Printing

Nasus Publishing
Minneapolis, MN 55337

How To Make Your Business Run Without You

Streamline Your Business Operations to Pave the Way for:
More Business, Bigger Profits
and a Business that Virtually Runs Itself!

Susan M. Carter

Published by:
Nasus Publishing
14209 Fountain Hills Court NE
Minneapolis, MN 55372
www.successideas.com

Copyright © 1999, 2001, 2002, 2003, 2004 by Susan Carter

Printed in the United State of America

Library of Congress Catalog Card Number: 99-90390

ISBN 0-9670291-0-4

First Printing 1999
Second Printing 2002
Third Printing 2004

With love, respect and gratitude I dedicate this book to my mom,
Florence Grupa, and in memory of my dad, Lucian Grupa.
Thank you for a lifetime of unconditional love and support.

Disclaimer

The purpose of this manual is to educate and inform readers of techniques and methods successfully used by small business owners. The author and Nasus Publishing shall have neither liability nor responsibility to any person or entity with respect to any loss or damage caused, or alleged to be caused, directly or indirectly by the information contained in this book.

Table of Contents

SECTION I: Business Definition

SECTION II: The Business of Doing Business

ADDENDUMS

Preface

Why I Wrote This Book

Since I left the corporate business world over ten years ago and struck out on my own as an independent contractor, I have been fortunate to realize several entrepreneurial goals. Initially these goals revolved around offering clients my writing, marketing and project management services. Armed with a naïve "I think I can" perspective, a handful of supportive, influential contacts (yes, sometimes it is 'who you know' that counts!) and a giant dose of luck, my little business survived.

Just one short year into my self-directed venture, I stumbled onto a segment of the business community that uses a very specific business model for success. As I learned more and more about the formula for this business model, and applied my writing and marketing skills to it, I discovered that I had developed a viable consulting practice that helps small businesses make the transition from start-up status to ongoing success.

Here is the short version of what I discovered:

Companies pay thousands of dollars for someone to come into their businesses to:

- *align the business owner's current business with his/her ideal business,*
- *study and assess the efficiency of current business procedures,*
- *examine alternate operating methods that would support the ideal business, improve efficiencies and boost profits,*
- *formulate repeatable procedures for effective and streamlined operations,*
- *document the business-enhancing method(s) used for every aspect of the operation into simple, easy-to-understand text, bound into an easily updateable format, that would serve as the company's personalized formula for business success.*

Often, that 'someone' who provided these services was me. So, who are these companies that will pay this kind of money for my services?

My initial clients were businesses preparing for franchise licensing. I discovered that franchise businesses use a very specific and methodical formula for organizing their operations. If you know anything about franchise businesses, you know each franchise store or service is set up to look and operate exactly the same as the next store or service for the same franchise. As an example, let's look at the grand daddy of all franchise businesses: McDonalds.

Walk into any McDonalds in any city (and just about any country!) and what do you see? Outside you see the famous golden arches. Inside you see plastic molded seating and employees dressed in uniforms. Behind the order counter is a big menu board with the same meal choices as any other McDonalds.

What do you get? You get whatever you can get at any other McDonalds. Hamburgers are made the same way. French fries are deep fried in the same temperature of oil, for the exact same amount of time as they are at the next McDonalds. Your order is bagged at one place in exactly the same manner as it is in the next.

Where is the owner? The owner is probably not present. Why?

A McDonalds franchise—and any other well-planned franchise—is set up as a turnkey business. A turnkey business is not owner-dependent nor is it people-dependent. A turnkey business is systems-dependent. There is a specific way (system) to perform every task to achieve repeatable, consistent results every time—with or without the owner's day-to-day involvement. I think that's a great way to run a business, don't you?

One thing that makes this systems-dependent formula so great is that it does not 'belong' solely to the franchise community. A business does not have to franchise in order to apply the franchise methods. If only one McDonalds existed, and it maintained the systems-dependent operation, it would still give repeatable performance and consistent results to its customers. And it would still be able to run without its owner present.

So here is the simple, basic pyramid of goals I outline and use with my client companies—both franchise and non-franchise:

A systems-dependent business =

Repeatable performance =

Consistent results =

A business that can virtually run itself!

My client list includes varied types of businesses and spans U.S. locations from Maryland, Kentucky, Wisconsin, and Minnesota to Missouri, North Dakota and Arizona. A business success formula works anywhere, with virtually any kind of business and with any size of business—from a one-person office to companies with 100's of employees.

In recent years I have connected with clients who have the sincere desire to make the "from start-up to ongoing success" transition themselves. They want to know how to assess their own businesses, develop consistent success-building operational methods, and create the supporting documentation manuals that will outline their personal success formulas. Since I can personally only handle a fairly small number of clients each year, I was eager to find resources that could help them take their personal efforts further.

I scoured the libraries and reference shelves for as much information as I could get my hands on that would help business owners capitalize on their do-it-yourself ambition. Guess what I found? Nothing. Nil. Zero. Zilch.

I found books on advertising, marketing, public relations, image development, and sales. I found motivational books, and books from the latest business gurus with professional insight and managerial strategies. I also found several books on 'how to buy a franchise' but none of these explained the "how to" for franchise business operations development and documentation.

Since I could not find a viable how-to resource to recommend to my clients, I decided to create it myself. After two years of thinking about it and formulating the process into a simplified version of my one-on-one consulting services, this book has become a reality. This do-it-yourself guide will step you through the basics for developing your own personal business success formula.

My job is, and always has been, to facilitate the extraction of a client's knowledge and document it into the company's personal business success formula. I do that by visiting a client's business, walking through the operation and asking questions — lots of them. Why are things done a certain way? How does that add to efficiency? If it doesn't, might there be a better way to streamline the process? What kind of growth is expected? What things will fluctuate as you grow; what things will stay the same regardless of your size?

I will be doing the same thing in the pages of this book. I will be asking the questions, probing for ways to look at your business from a new perspective. I'll pose the same questions in these pages that I would ask if we were sitting face to face in your office.

Here's the really *great* news.

No one knows your business better than you do.

- YOU have all the knowledge.
- YOU have the strategy and foresight.
- YOU have all the answers about what's working and what isn't working.
- YOU have the solutions!

Through the information I provide in these pages, I am able to do two things:

1. Service the many clients who have been 'on hold' simply because I couldn't immediately take on new business.
2. Give other business owners an opportunity to see their businesses from a new perspective and offer a time-tested "how to" process to help them achieve what every owner strives for — a business that virtually runs itself.

That is why I wrote this book.

Introduction

What's In It For You?
How to Get More Than Your Money's Worth from This Book

Let's jump right to the bottom line: what's in it for you? What will your reward be for spending the time (and money) on this book?

If all you do is simply read this book, you will walk away with information and ideas that will positively impact the future success of your business. You will gain a new perspective on how to remove yourself from the day-to-day involvement owners are notorious for, even after they've hired people who supposedly will take daily responsibilities from them.

However, if you want to get the most you possibly can out of the pages of this book, reading it is not enough. This is not a book of theory, it is a book of instruction. You must become an active participant. The value is not in *me telling you* what to do; the value is in the doing. The more time and effort you put into reading each chapter, answering the questions and applying these techniques to your own business, the more valuable this information will be to you.

The organization methods described in this book are designed to remove an owner from the day-to-day involvement of running a business. The goal is to create a systems-dependent business that can efficiently run without the daily, physical presence of the owner. However, these same methods can be applied to a professional services business in which the owner is the sole service provider, such as a dentist, chiropractor, veterinarian, etc. In these businesses, the owner is in the office, but must remain free of interruptions when with a customer/client. A systems-dependent, self-supporting method of organization can be critical to maintain quality of care.

Once you've documented a consistent way of handling all business situations, you will immediately know the answers to the tough questions. You will become less scattered in your thought process and stop 'reinventing the wheel' every time you deal with a customer or vendor.

Once you set the tone for consistency, your clients will see it in the way you do business with them. Your employees will show it by knowing what you expect of them. You will notice your business running smoother with fewer 'loose ends' to tie up at the end of each day. And you will be free to take more time for yourself, and/or spend time on increasing business to bring in more profit.

By exercising both patience and persistence to apply these methods, you can realize a measurable and profitable return on your investment that will serve you well as your business develops and grows.

To get the most from this book, I encourage you to do the following:

- Make an "uninterrupted" time investment. This might mean blocking out the first (or last) two hours of every day to dedicate to Making Your Business Run Without You. Or, if you are at a point in your business where you cannot afford to be unreachable for that length of time, it may mean coming in early or staying late in order to get through a chapter at a time.

- To maintain momentum, schedule your uninterrupted time as though it were an appointment with yourself. Write it in your appointment book. Don't change it unless it is absolutely necessary and, if you must change it, don't just 'skip' it for the day — reschedule it. Make it just as important as the appointments you keep with your customers and your family and friends.

- Answer questions as thoroughly as possible. If you put all of the effort you possibly can into completing the exercises in Section I of this book, the documentation for Section II of this book will be easier.

- When instructed to answer questions or complete an exercise, describe/explain a procedure, etc., do it in a word processing program. If you don't type — or your brain freezes at the thought of 'writing' — then dictate your thoughts and answers into a tape recorder and have someone else transcribe those thoughts into a word processing program. Why? As mentioned in the previous point, much of the information you are gathering in Section I of this book will become the basis for documentation you'll be asked to develop in Section II. Get as much as you possibly can saved into a text file that can be edited later.

- Carry a small spiral notebook or a small tape recorder with you to make notes during times you aren't specifically working on the information. Once you begin this process, you will think of ideas during conversations with associates, while attending meetings, at the dinner table, or socializing with friends. Make sure you have some way to record your thoughts.

If you enter into this process with the same enthusiasm and dedication you needed to start your business, you will find the same satisfaction and reward when you turn the final page of this book.

Keep your eye on the prize: *a business that will virtually run without you!*

Chapter 1

Why Your Business MUST Be Able to Run Without You

The single most important reason why your business *must* be able to run without you is, quite simply: **RISK**. The more your business success is dependent on your personal day-to-day involvement, the more you put your business at risk to falter and fail.

I've experienced the same frustration that you may be experiencing now. Just like mine, many businesses are owner-operated with few — if any — employees. You take an idea from concept to reality and carefully carve a plan for implementation. It succeeds. Customers want what you have. You are able to fill their needs. Your business is on the success track. Yet, as business increases, control begins to disintegrate. You realize that, having implemented a great start-up plan, you did not plan for the next level of growth. Suddenly you are consumed by the daily tasks that must be performed to take care of your increasing customer base. While you are diligently working **IN** the business to keep things afloat, it is inevitable that there is an increasing neglect to working **ON** the business.

Whether you are that same owner-operator who started his/her business several years ago, or a business with 10, 50 or 100 employees, many owners remain caught in the same "catch 22" situation. You are unable to detach yourself from the daily tasks, and unable to spend the necessary time orchestrating the next level of success. Although you may not be slipping backwards, it's evident you are also not going forward. You have reached a critical point in determining the future success of your business.

Once your business becomes motionless, it is difficult to get the momentum back. Opportunities are lost while you struggle to maintain your ground. And by the time you are able to regain your footing, you cannot recapture the business you've lost, or sent away, because you were unable to accommodate the new demands.

By doing what is necessary NOW, you can significantly reduce the risk of potential problems that can quickly gain momentum and lead to possible—and probable—failure.

How to Eliminate Small Business Vulnerability

Statistics from the Small Business Administration (SBA) show that, in 1997, there were 1,284,333 new businesses and incorporations formed. Those same statistics state that there were 994,283 closures, bankruptcies and terminations in 1997. That means, for every four new businesses that opened their doors, three established businesses closed theirs. Supporting data from the Bureau of the Census shows over 99.9 percent of business closures are small firms (as defined by the SBA, small firms employ 500 or fewer employees).

In recent years I've read that, if a business can survive its first three years, its chances for success increase. Some say it's five years (others say seven years) that determines the success-ability factor for any new business. Regardless of the length of time that tests an individual company's success, the cause of the above closure statistics can primarily be categorized into one of these four challenges:

1. **Financial resources**. A company does not have the financial resources to maintain current inventory or personnel; or, cannot convince a bank to invest in growth.

2. **The compromise of acquisition**. The worth of a business is determined by how valuable a commodity it is to another company for a merger or acquisition, rather than its value as a stand alone business.

3. **Drastic changes in the market demand for products or services.** When demand for a company's product/ service diminishes—with little or no chance of returning—it will put the company out of business. For example, if a company makes typewriters and the market is demanding computers, the market has significantly changed and directly affects potential for success selling typewriters.

4. **Transition planning deficit**. Failure to map out a strategy to take the business from "start up" status to a "growing" business can be devastating to long term goals and prevents a business from increasing potential for greater success and more profit.

Ironically, items 1, 2, and 3 above are directly related to item 4. Without planning for transition from a "start up" business to a "growing" business, a company's financial resources will be depleted or chances for new resources will be diminished.

Without planning for transition, an owner may be able to establish a business that is attractive as a buy-out for another company, but does that compromise the value of the business according to the company's initial plan? And, if a company doesn't see—and plan for—the inevitable market changes directly affecting the future of the business, then the company is lacking in the transition planning that must exist to remain competitive.

By concentrating on a strategy for taking your business from start-up status to ongoing success and growth, companies are in a position to eliminate their vulnerability. Yet, by reviewing the above stated opening/closure statistics, many businesses are either not focused on strategy—or simply don't know where to begin.

Having said that, I have another interesting statistic from the U.S. Department of Commerce: <u>95 percent of all franchise businesses succeed</u>. Typically, franchise businesses are small businesses. They don't have any more influence on customers than your business. So what catapults their success rate to 95 percent?

The requirements imposed on a franchise in order to become licensed include the strategies, operations enhancement tactics and procedural documentation to be presented as a turnkey system. This turnkey system is so clearly defined, there is no division between start-up status and ongoing success. The entire process is predetermined and incorporated into the business operation at the onset. <u>With the implementation of this system, the business is able to run without the owner</u> and becomes a marketable commodity.

The success of the franchisor—the parent company—comes from the ability to develop the strategy and procedures for the turnkey business. The franchisor works **ON** the business, developing the blueprint for others to follow to achieve the same success, in the same way, as the parent company does. The franchisee (franchise buyer) works **IN** the business and uses the success formula devised by the franchisor.

Your business does not have to become a franchise to benefit from the success-building tactics used by franchisors. Every one of you can assume the role of "franchisor." Regardless of whether you have one single location with the same number of employees you've always had, or decide to branch into other locations, departments or subsidiaries, in the role of franchisor you will constantly be working **ON** your business, not in it. For your business to continue to grow and remain profitable, it must be able to run without you. This is accomplished by developing the turnkey system that fits your individual goals, taking your direct involvement out of the day-to-day operational tasks.

Increase Your Company's Success By Emulating Successful Franchise Techniques

For nearly ten years I have been helping businesses — both franchise and non-franchise — develop the necessary strategies, operations changes and procedural documentation to transform a good, solid business concept into a self-sufficient turnkey company. I want to do the same for you through the writing of this book. By emulating how a franchise business prepares for success you, too, can achieve consistent, predictable results for your business. You can turn your business into a turnkey operation, governed by a set of success-building procedures that will virtually allow your business to run without you.

This is a "how to" book and I take that definition literally. The information in this book is not steeped in lengthy theories and concepts with the emphasis on "what" to do. A how-to book should not only tell you "what" to do but "how" to do it. That's what you'll find in these pages.

I'll use stories to illustrate specific points and I will be talking with you the same way I do when I'm one-on-one with my clients. I'll be asking you the same questions I ask them. I'll give examples to demonstrate how implementing small changes can achieve big results. I'll step you through a logical progression of actions to take your business from start-up status to consistent, ongoing success.

What's Ahead

Chapters 2 and 3 demonstrate the importance of consistency in your business — both for your internal operations as they relate to your employees and for the operations as they relate to your customers. Please do not skip these two chapters! The foundation of a systems-dependent business is built on consistency.

Chapter 4 begins the first of two hands-on sections where you'll begin the work for your own business-building formula. Section I focuses on the business of defining (or redefining) your business and the ultimate goals you must identify for its future success. I'll prompt you to rethink and reevaluate how your business currently runs, and show you how to bridge today's reality to tomorrow's vision. I'll show you how to separate yourself from day-to-day involvement and take your rightful place as owner. I'll talk about employee relationships and why hiring the inexperienced can work to your advantage.

Chapter 10 is the introduction for Section II. Section II focuses on the business of doing business — documentation. Once you've determined your business goals and how to attain them through consistent procedures, you must have a blueprint to document the success formula. In the game of football, we'd call it the play book. In the art of cooking and baking, we'd call it the recipe. In business we call it the operations manual and, just like in football and cooking, if you try to follow the system without documenting the steps in the process, you're setting yourself up to fail. You may get it right some of the time, but "some of the time" is rarely good enough to establish and keep loyal fans, patrons or customers. I'll also share proven methods for eliminating redundancies that will help to streamline your operation to increase efficiency, productivity and profits.

By the time you turn the last page of this book, you will have the business tools to:

- *Align your current business with your ideal business so your company can grow into the business you intended it to be,*
- *Objectively evaluate what's working for your business, what's not, and what to do about it,*
- *Detect the profit-eaters of your business and transformed them into profit-enhancers,*
- *Streamline your business operations to pave the way for more new business and increased repeat business,*

- *Eliminate the destructive results of high employee turnover, procedural redundancy and lost opportunities,*

- *Prepare a comprehensive operations manual that documents your company's success formula and provides your customers with consistent services and products that keep them coming back for more,*

- *Develop a turnkey business that virtually runs itself, giving you more time to work ON your business instead of IN your business.*

Over the years, many of my clients have told me that two of their biggest challenges are motivating employees and acquiring financial assistance. That's why I've included two special addendums at the back of this book.

The first addendum is entitled "5 Creative Employee Motivators." It outlines five ways to turn apathetic "it's just a job" employees into superstars who help your company get to its next profit level.

The second addendum is a Financial Aid Resource Guide listing people and organizations you can turn to for raising capital for start-up or expansion. I've also included a glossary of definitions for various types of financing options, and advice on how to increase your odds for getting the cash you need.

If you're serious about taking the first step to making your business run without you, turn the page and let's get started!

Chapter Notes & Ideas

Chapter 2

How To Handle Growth So It Will "Make" Your Business Rather Than "Break" Your Business

This chapter begins with a fictitious story to demonstrate the effects of growth on a start-up business. While the actual story is fictitious, it depicts common challenges typically encountered by small business owners.

Meet Paul Planworthy.

Paul is an ambitious, entrepreneurial person. While still in high school, he excelled in math and sciences and also enjoyed shop classes where he was able to work with production machines. This was a dynamite skill combination for success in the manufacturing industry. Paul became a student intern at a local machine shop, DoHickey & Sons, during his junior and senior years.

Dilbert and Delia DoHickey, the husband and wife owners of DoHickey & Sons, quickly recognized the boy's talent and offered him an apprenticeship with the company throughout his technical school training years. Paul was eager to learn every machine and every technique used in the shop to make the best quality products in the market.

After his apprenticeship, Paul was hired as a full time employee of the company. He continued to focus on making the best products possible. He learned every aspect of each machine to maximize production. He devised specific processes that improved the company's shop floor operations. Paul took pride in what he could do, and his perseverance for perfection paid off in loyal, satisfied customers for DoHickey and Sons.

Then things changed.

Dilbert and Delia, in their quest to retire, handed the management reigns to their two "Sons" of DoHickey & Sons. Focused on increasing profits (and bigger paychecks for themselves), Dufus and Dreyfus began to find ways to shorten machining times by "cutting corners" in some of the processes used for product manufacture. Paul, the perfectionist, watched product quality quickly decline, and soon became disenchanted with his employment by DoHickey & Sons.

Paul's pleas to Dilbert and Delia to influence Dufus and Dreyfus fell on sympathetic ears, but to no avail. Although they were disappointed that the sons had changed the business—and its reputation—the elder DoHickeys also acknowledged they gave up control. The success or failure of the business was in their sons' hands. Knowing of Paul's high standards and integrity, Dilbert and Delia encouraged him to "do what you have to do" even if it meant competing against their sons.

Paul, knowing he could employ the same entrepreneurial spirit he used to help DoHickey thrive, decided to open his own shop. Perfectionist trait in tact, he carefully prepared a business plan, complete with capital expenditures and profit projections. He also acquired and presented signed testimonies from several DoHickey customers who said they would give Paul their business if he were to set up his own shop. A letter from the elder DoHickeys also attested to Paul's knowledge and entrepreneurial traits. Paul was granted the loan and Paul's Perfect Parts Inc. was born.

Paul's business thrived. He was proud to be in charge of his own destiny. He considered himself a successful entrepreneur.

For two years Paul worked diligently in his business. He eventually hired a receptionist, Mandy, who was kept busy with phone duties, filing, mailings, and greeting visitors. She was eager to help Paul, and often asked to be given more responsibility. Paul, in his efforts to maintain the quality of the shop, did all of the estimating, scheduled work through the shop, and ran the jobs himself. He invested in state-of-the-art equipment that would give him maximum return on his investment and keep him current in the industry, able to compete for jobs that a less-equipped shop could attain. His one-man operation was rewarded with satisfied customers who knew they could count on his work quality and personal integrity.

By year three, Paul's Perfect Parts Inc. was gaining momentum. A healthy economy and several mergers graced Paul with more work from current customers. Word of mouth about his excellent shop was bringing in new business. Paul was now working 14-hour days, six days a week to keep up with the volume of work and delivery promises. Knowing he could no longer handle all of the work himself, Paul hired a machinist named Biff Foolhearty, formerly of DoHickey & Sons, who had once come to him asking if there might be a spot for him in Paul's company.

Relieved to have another experienced, capable machinist to help with the work, Paul felt things were back under control. To have someone with previous shop experience working for him was a comfort to Paul. The two of them worked side by side and kept the workflow manageable. Biff would help with the quotes and shop scheduling and Paul could concentrate on researching and devising new ways to make the shop more efficient, productive and profitable. Paul was also able to enjoy an occasional three-day weekend with his now growing family.

Suddenly, everything changed — again.

It was the first Monday in February of Paul's fourth year in business. Paul's biggest customer, Whachama Dinger Industries, had faxed cancellation notices of three jobs.

Paul was stunned. He quickly called the customer to find out what had happened. As he listened in disbelief to the customer's tale of receiving many promises with no follow-through, Paul knew his reputation was fast becoming compromised.

After a lengthy discussion with the customer, it soon became clear to Paul that Biff was at the root of the mounting problems. Biff was making promises that were impossible to keep and, with each delay, the customer lost confidence in the company as a reliable supplier. Paul promised the customer he would personally handle all three jobs and extend a substantial discount on all three orders if he would reconsider and void the cancellation notices. The customer, who knew Paul would keep his word, agreed.

Paul confronted Biff on the shop floor. Without even turning away from the job he was currently machining, Biff responded, "It's not my fault the quote was sent out with a delivery date we couldn't make. Talk to Mandy."

Paul said, "Mandy? Our receptionist? She doesn't know how to configure quotes!"

Biff replied, "She never told me she couldn't do it. When I asked her to finish plugging in the numbers and delivery, she just said, 'okay' — how was I to know she didn't know what she was doing? Besides, I've got more than enough to do here on the shop floor just getting these machines to spit out parts. I don't have time to review the work she does."

Paul couldn't believe what he was hearing. "Didn't I tell you when I hired you that, if you had any questions or problems, you should come to ME?"

Biff simply replied, "I didn't have any questions or problems. Mandy said she would handle it."

Mandy was finishing a phone call with one of the company's vendors as Paul sat down in one of the chairs facing her desk in the reception area. She was great with people on the phone. He always heard comments from customers and vendors at how pleasant it is to call this office. This was going to be a tough conversation.

When Mandy hung up the phone, Paul recounted the phone call he'd had with the customer and the subsequent conversation with Biff. He ended by asking, "Is what Biff tells me true?"

Mandy, sheepishly admitted it was.

"What ever made you think you would be able to finish a customer quote and establish a delivery date?" he asked.

"I've seen hundreds of them go through this office. And I've heard you with vendors and watched how you put the numbers together," she said. "I looked up some of the old tickets and modeled the quotes after those."

"Mandy," said Paul, "the new quotes weren't for reruns of previous — or even similar — parts! These are entirely new parts with multiple processes. That takes more time to do and new costs have to be determined."

"I'm so sorry, Paul," Mandy says, with tears beginning to well in her eyes. "When Biff asked if I could do it, I thought it would be a chance to show you I could do more around here besides answer phones and file. I thought I was helping you!"

This kind of help from well-meaning employees could quickly be the downfall of Paul's Perfect Parts. Paul needed to get back the control of his business and he saw only one solution. He made it clear to both Biff and Mandy that absolutely everything was to come to him first. He would do all of the quotes. He would set the schedule and oversee production, and he would follow up with the customers and vendors. He couldn't count on his employees to do it right so, the only way he could be sure it was being done right, was to do it himself.

Unfortunately, Paul is right back where he started: putting more work IN his business than ON his business. He has employees but, in order for everything to be done right, he will once again have to focus on the day-to-day operations.

What went wrong? Better yet, what can be done to make it go right?

Planning Doesn't End When Your Doors Open for Business

Paul didn't plan to fail. Paul failed to plan. While it is true that Paul planned extensively before he went into business, he failed to plan for growth. More specifically, he failed to plan for training employees who would contribute to growth.

Mandy had excellent organization and people skills. Biff was a skilled machinist. Paul made wise choices for the employees he needed. His only error was in not training Mandy and Biff to do things the way he wanted them done *in his shop*. This one error nearly cost him his largest customer. Losing his largest customer could have devastated his business.

Paul assumed Biff's experience came bundled with common sense. It didn't. The only valuable experience Biff was able to bring to Paul's business was as a machinist. Everything else Biff knew about business was learned from his previous employer. And at DoHickey and Sons, Biff learned that the receptionist took care of generating customer quotes. Since Biff knew Paul began his career at DoHickey and Sons, he had no reason to believe quotes were handled any other way.

And what about Mandy? Perhaps she should have known better than to attempt quoting customer jobs, but since Biff was the one who approached her, she believed he had the authority to allow her to do the quote. This assumption was a direct result of Paul's lack of clarification when Biff was hired. Biff was introduced to Mandy as Paul's "right hand man" – why wouldn't she believe Biff had the authority to give her additional responsibilities?

The unfortunate results of this scenario all comes down to the damaging effects of making assumptions: Paul *assumed* both Biff and Mandy would know what to do. They didn't.

Does any of this sound familiar? Do you have similar miscommunications and people taking on jobs they aren't capable of doing? Do you assume employees come with a certain kind of common sense or instinct that will be an asset to your business? Could growth be the beginning of the end for you, too?

Employees come equipped with talent and skill. How those talents and skills are applied in your specific business is up to you to communicate to them. In order to achieve the results you want you must develop procedures (a system) that will give you consistent results.

Regardless of the type of business you have, if it lacks consistency, variations of Paul's story will begin to surface in your own company. If you aren't prepared to train people to do things your way using your own specific system of procedures, growth could **break** your business. If you are prepared to train people to do things your way using a well-planned, well-documented 'blueprint' for successful results, growth can **make** your business.

Chapter Notes & Ideas

Chapter 3

The Quest for Consistency and Why It Is the Most Important Aspect of a Successful Business

Have you ever heard of any of these businesses: *McDonald's, H&R Block, Century 21, Dairy Queen, ServiceMaster, Dollar Rent a Car, Holiday Inn, Taco Bell, Midas Muffler, Roto Rooter, Pearle Vision, Mail Boxes Etc., PIP Printing, Culligan Water Conditioning, Domino's Pizza?* These businesses are just a few of the currently top rated 100 franchises.

Yet, as I mentioned in the *Preface* of this book, the fact that they are franchise businesses is not what makes them successful. Success is not inherent in the act of franchising the business, but rather in the formula owners use in organizing and operating the business as a turnkey system. And the power of this franchise formula can be applied to any business, any time, anywhere to achieve maximum productivity — and profitability. By emulating the strategies used by successful franchises, you, too, can harness the power and apply it to drive the ongoing success of your business.

So what is this 'secret power' that drives these businesses to success?

Consistency.

That's it! One word. The one thing every franchise business owner provides to its customers is consistency. And in the proper execution of action to attain this one thing, an owner not only creates a turnkey, streamlined business that keeps customers coming back again and again, but s/he also creates the foundation for a business that successfully runs without her/him!

Consistency is NOT Synonymous with Superiority

I want you to notice the word consistency does not mean 'the best' or indicate the highest quality. According to the *American Heritage Dictionary* definition, consistency is:

Reliability or uniformity of successive results or events.

In our competitive business world, it is nearly impossible for any one company to strive for and achieve ranking as the 'best' at what it does or sells. Many companies would be out of business if people only patronized businesses delivering 'the best' products and services.

Successful companies know customer satisfaction comes from giving customers what you tell them you're going to give them, and giving it to them consistently. As in the definition above, the thing to strive for is 'reliability or uniformity'.

Before you start writing your letters to me defending the glories of striving to be the best, let me illustrate this point by again referring to our well-known franchise leader: McDonald's.

Be honest. Does McDonald's make the BEST hamburger you've ever tasted? Some of you may answer 'yes' but I suspect most of you will answer 'no'. To simply have a difference of opinion tells us that defining and declaring the 'best' of any product or service is highly objective and personal.

In fact, McDonald's does not *claim* to make the best hamburger. Nor do they claim to make the best french fries or milk shakes. So why do we as customers choose to go to McDonald's?

We go to McDonald's because we know exactly what to expect. We know what we're going to get. If you order a Big Mac, it will taste exactly the same as the one you ordered last week and the week before. You are never disappointed. You know what to expect and that's exactly what you get.

You can rely on McDonald's to give you what they always give you: Consistency.

While we're on the subject of McDonald's, let me ask you this…where is the owner?

Taking your order? No.

Flipping burgers? No.

Standing watch over the employees? Rarely.

The owner is usually not present. Why? Because there is a turnkey *system* in place that creates and ensures consistency. The owner does not need to be on the premises for the business to succeed.

And that's what you want for your business.

Why Consistency Is the Most Important Aspect of Your Business

The power of the franchise business success formula (consistency) can be applied to any business. And the benefits gained from the structure associated with this formula can keep your business at 'the top of its game' year after year.

You achieve consistency by doing the same thing in the same way so it produces exactly the same results each and every time you do it. You want your customers to know exactly what they can expect from you. They rely on you to give it to them each and every time they do business with you.

For your customers to be able to expect consistency of service or product, you must be able to identify the elements that go into consistency. Once identified, should consistency be compromised, you will easily be able to pinpoint where that deviation occurred and immediately be able to get back on course.

Let's look at this from the customer perspective.

I have a friend who begins every morning by frequenting the same gourmet coffee shop. She takes her morning paper, orders coffee and a breakfast muffin, and sits at one of the bistro-style tables (preferably near the window!).

There's a reason she goes to the same place every day: she knows what to expect. She knows the counter person will greet her pleasantly, announce the daily specialty blend, serve her quickly and thank her as she leaves. The coffee she orders will taste the same, be made the same, be the right drinking temperature, and it will be served in a sturdy cup and not too hot to hold. She knows if she turns to her right she'll find the counter that holds the creamer, sugar, stir sticks and napkins. She knows when she sits at the table, it will be clean, uncluttered, and have additional napkins, etc. for her use.

Small as they may seem, these things are important to her. She relies on the consistent product and service of this coffee shop. If she had to go back to the counter and ask for creamer because it wasn't available on the service counter, she would be annoyed. If she sat at the table and there were crumbs and sugar spritzes from the person who sat there before her, she would be annoyed. If the coffee cup was so thin that it would be impossible to handle, she would be annoyed. All of these small, seemingly insignificant annoyances would eventually lead her to the doorway of another coffee shop.

Here's what I want you to remember: The coffee she buys is not the 'product' being delivered. Dozens of coffee houses are scattered in the neighborhood. She is buying consistent performance.

My friend knows exactly what to expect when she goes to this coffee shop—a good cup of coffee she enjoys, in a polished, quaint and pleasant atmosphere. This coffee shop satisfies this expectation on a daily basis and she is not disappointed.

Here's the point. **Consistency creates the reputation your business will be built on.** Without it, you will constantly be learning from mistakes that you can't afford to make. Customers will walk away without telling you why. One to three years will pass from your Grand Opening day to your Going Out of Business day and you will not understand what happened.

Your business success formula must detail every element necessary to create consistency. If you do the same thing in exactly the same way every time you do it, you will get the same results. Each day. Every day.

By documenting procedures in detail, and following them, you set your plan for methodical success rather than haphazard hit and miss luck. For you to deliver to the customer exactly what you say you're going to deliver, you must provide consistency.

Okay, I can already hear some of you saying, "But, Susan, my business thrives on an ability to be creative and innovative." Don't miss the point stated earlier: **"Consistency creates the reputation your business will be built on."** Consistency is the foundation of "the business of doing business" and does not interfere with creativity and innovation.

Many years ago I worked as a writer in an ad agency. We were expected to create ads for our clients. Despite the client expectation for creative results, we had a *methodology* for developing those ads. Primarily we conducted brainstorming sessions with other staff members using the 'green light' method where no one was allowed to criticize another's suggestion—every idea was put on the chalkboard regardless of how silly someone else thought it sounded.

The green light session is a methodology. It did not hinder creativity or innovation. It was a method used to achieve the desired creative results. An outline of how one is conducted is in the agency's business success formula (operations manual).

We also had procedures for acquiring clients, working with clients, presenting to clients and executing the use of a multitude of forms to process the work—between clients, between writing/graphic staff, between placement vendors, etc. Although there was a creative nature to our business, there was still the need for the "business of doing business" to be methodical and consistent.

If you, the business owner, cannot check on the status of any project at any given time, something is awry in your business operations. Things will start to fall between the cracks and you will never be able to remedy the problem if you don't know how to track the project.

So if consistency is so important to business success, how do you develop it and where do you begin?

Good question!

It begins with you starting Chapter 4!

SECTION I:

Business Definition

Chapter 4

What Business Are You In?
The Art of Niche Marketing and Why It Is Important to Your Success

How do you identify your business? When people ask you, 'what do you do?', what do you say? If you are like most of us we define our business by the industry we're in. "I have a children's clothing shop," or, "I own an auto repair shop," or "I'm a computer consultant," or, "I'm a pet groomer."

Yet, what your customers go home with (toddlers clothes, a new fan belt, new software or a new "do" for Fu-Fu) is the end result of a much greater part of your business—your image. It is often the only thing that sets any of us apart from our competitors. Why?

People are emotional buyers. They come to a certain place, or buy from a certain company because of the way they feel when they enter the business location or talk with employees. Customers will make both conscious and unconscious buying decisions based on:

1. The way a business looks,
2. The way employees treat them,
3. How well you keep the promises you make to them.

1. The way a business looks.

It doesn't matter if you physically have a store or office location, spend most of your time going to the customer's location, or do all of your business via a web site. When you are in a position to give people a visual impression, you will be judged by what they see. It might be the décor of your retail shop or office. It might be the way you dress when you meet your customer for the first time at his/her location. Or it might be the layout design and organization of your web site. First impressions count. They are a reflection of you and the way you conduct business. Is the first impression you make on customers one that reflects a professional and polished business, or a scattered and chaotic business?

2. The way your employees treat them.

We all communicate in various ways. Words, gestures, tone of voice and body language used by you and your employees send multiple messages to your potential customers. What you say and how you say it will either invite customers to do business with you, or communicate that their business is not your top priority. Do you and your employees enthusiastically greet your customers, or do you appear to be annoyed because it is an interruption of your day?

3. How well you keep the promises you make to them.

When customers give you the opportunity to earn their business, make sure you deliver on your promises. Never make a promise you can't keep! When a customer orders something from you, give him/her a realistic delivery date. If there is an unforeseen delay, immediately let the customer know about it. If you claim to sell something that is 'the best' or 'the fastest' or 'the sturdiest' or 'the softest' or 'the most powerful' of all its competitors, then it better be or the customer might never do business with you again. Whether you sell products or services, the best way to turn a new customer into a repeat customer is to undersell and overdeliver.

The Advantages of Defining a Niche Market

Who is your customer?

If you are an auto repair shop, for instance, you might answer, "my customer is anyone with a vehicle!" If you own a crafts supply store, you might say, "my customer is anyone who likes to make crafts." If you are a bookkeeper, you might answer, "anyone who needs book work done."

While these 'one size fits all' answers are certainly true, you are not clearly differentiating yourself from your competitors. You are not creating a specific reason for a potential customer to choose your business over another.

The best way to illustrate my point is to put *you* in the customer's shoes.

Let's say you are the proud owner of a brand new puppy. And let's say the puppy is a cocker spaniel you've named Jezebel. As your puppy grows, she needs to have her claws trimmed and her coat clipped and cleaned. After talking with your veterinarian, you find out there are three pet grooming businesses in town. Your vet also tells you they are equally competent groomers. How do you decide which one to use?

You might start by simply looking in the yellow pages of the phone book to find out where each of the groomers is located and to get their phone numbers.

You notice the three listings for the shops the veterinarian mentioned, which read like this:

(Shop #1)

> **Pampered Paws Salon**: We specialize in award winning clips for award winning dogs.

(Shop #2)

> **Personal Touch Pet Grooming**: We treat man's best friend just like family! Service while you wait in our child-friendly waiting room!

(Shop #3)

> **Pet Pals Grooming** — the place to go for all of your pet grooming needs.

Based solely on these ads, have you already been influenced about which one to choose? In reality, all of them perform the same service. And, according to the veterinarian, each one performs it as well as the next. Yet, depending on your plans for your new cocker spaniel, you may already have consciously or unconsciously made your choice for a groomer.

Do you envision Jezebel becoming a show dog? Or is she going to be the family pet? By claiming a specialty, and projecting that IMAGE in a simple yellow pages ad, the first two advertisers will most likely gain specific business. The Pampered Paws Salon will attract people who are interested in grooming their dogs for shows and contests. At Personal Touch Grooming, it's clear they understand how attached your children are to their new pet and the shop will treat her accordingly.

What about Pet Pals Grooming? Well, the ad says they can take care of all your grooming needs. But wouldn't you prefer a groomer who takes care of your *specific* needs? The 'we can do it all' approach simply leaves the potential customer flat.

It is likely that shops #1 and 2 get most of the business simply because they are targeting a specific niche market. You, too, will attract more business if you define a specific type of customer (a niche market) and directly market your products or services to that niche.

Who do you want your primary customers to be? Once you decide, then you must do everything you can to attract those customers! Find out what they want. Then give it to them!

Every good business is built on filling a customer need.

Every great business is built on filling a customer need in a very specific way.

How to Develop a Consistent Image

The way your business looks, everything you do and say, and how you and your employees act and react, must revolve around serving your niche customer. And all of these things must be consistent each and every time a new customer or repeat customer walks into your place of business or calls you on the phone.

Let me illustrate this by continuing with the pet grooming example.

Since there are only three groomers in town, you decide to make a phone call to each shop to find out the rates, the hours it is open for business, how far in advance you need to make an appointment, etc. Conversations go something like this:

Shop #1:

Receptionist: "Good morning, Pampered Paws Salon, this is Lisa."

You: "Good morning, Lisa. I'm calling to find out your rates and business hours."

Receptionist: "Our regular hours are from 10 a.m. to 7 p.m. Monday through Saturday, but we also accommodate additional hours by appointment. Our rates vary depending on the services you'd like. How can we serve you on your first visit with us?

You: "I need to have my puppy's claws trimmed and probably her first bath."

Receptionist: We like to start puppies out with the royal treatment! Our premiere dog bathing service includes a pre-bath comb out to remove any loose hair, a shampoo using a gentle product that does not dry out the skin, and a towel dry followed by a low heat blow dry and brush out to bring the shine back to the coat. The bath service is $30.00 and nail clipping is free.

You: "How far in advance do I need to make an appointment?"

Receptionist: "We make every effort to accommodate your schedule. When would be most convenient for you?

You: "I was thinking about Friday morning, but I am not quite ready to commit to an appointment. I will need to call back to schedule one."

Receptionist: "Well, we'll look forward to hearing from you. If you have any other questions, please call back."

Shop #2:

Receptionist: "Thank you for calling Personal Touch Pet Grooming. This is Janice, how may I help you?"

You: "Good morning, Janice. I'm calling to find out your rates and business hours."

Receptionist: "I'd be happy to provide that information. May I ask your pet's name and the kind of service you are interested in?

You: "Jezebel is our new cocker spaniel puppy and I need to have her claws trimmed and probably her first bath."

Receptionist: "We'd love to introduce Jezebel to her first bath! In fact we have a special Welcome Package for every new puppy that comes into our shop. It includes a claw trim, a bath using a gentle 'no tears' puppy shampoo, a thorough dry out and puppy's first tail trim. The Welcome Package is just $25.00. Also, after you've brought Jezebel in for five baths, the sixth one is free. Can I schedule Jezebel for an appointment this week?

You: "Not at this time. I will need to call back to set an appointment. What are your hours?"

Receptionist: "We are open every day from 9 a.m. to 7 p.m., including Saturday and Sunday. However, we will also open whatever additional hours are needed to accommodate your schedule.

You: "Thank you."

Receptionist: "Thank you for calling. We hope to meet Jezebel soon!"

Shop #3:

Receptionist: "Good morning, Pet Pals Grooming"

You: "Good morning, I'm calling to find out your rates and business hours."

Receptionist: "We're open Monday through Friday from 10 a.m. to 7 p.m. and on Saturdays from 9 a.m. to 5 p.m. Rates depend on what you want to have done."

You: "I need to have my puppy's claws trimmed and probably her first bath."

Receptionist: "Okay, let's see. The rate card says that trimming claws is $10.00 and a bath is $15.00."

You: "How far in advance do I need to make an appointment?"

Receptionist: "Sometimes it can be the same day. It just depends on how busy the shop is. Right now, we're pretty backed up and it looks like the next open appointment is next Tuesday at 3:15."

You: "All right. Thank you."

Receptionist: "You're welcome. Thank you for calling Pet Pals Grooming."

In all three of these examples, you receive the information you wanted. Yet, because of the way the phone call was handled, you are left with the impression (image) that Shop #1 is a bit upscale with their "premiere bathing service" and wanting to give Jezebel the 'royal treatment'.

What impression did you have of Shop #2? The receptionist asked for the pet's name and used it throughout the conversation. Does that make you feel like they care about her personally? The bathing services they offer are bundled as a "Welcome Package." Does that support a friendly, homey atmosphere?

Now, how did you feel about Shop #3? Clearly the receptionist needed to refer to a rate card to give you pricing. And while the pricing is similar to the other shops, there is no special package offered as an incentive. Also, shops #1 and #2 made it very clear they would make every effort to accommodate your schedule. Shop #3 simply stated the next available appointment time.

These may be seemingly small differences, but they can make a huge impact on results. Let's review potential decision-making scenarios:

Some of you may make your decision based on the ads alone—a niche market is identified and you identify with that niche. You will call the 'specialist' for the grooming services you prefer.

Others of you may decide based on both the ads and these initial phone conversations. <u>These decisions are primarily based on the way the employee (or it could even be the shop's owner) handled the phone call.</u> Still others of you may decide to physically check out the shops for yourselves. So, let's do that.

Shop #1 is a stand-alone building located one block from the biggest shopping mall in town. The building and signage is elegant, and tastefully constructed. A carport canopy extends from the entrance so patrons may drive to the doorway and drop off their pets during inclement weather.

When entering the shop, there is a row of chairs to the left that extends in a semi-circle around the corner of the wall. A low 'coffee table' extends in front of the seating. On the table are magazines about pets and pet products, and a "winners circle" book of photos of properly groomed show dogs. Beautiful artwork is displayed on the walls. A "best in breed" show announcement is posted on the glass-encased bulletin board. It is artfully arranged along with several professional photographs of previous winners that had been groomed by this particular salon. Behind the desk sits an employee dressed in a white lab coat with an embroidered logo on the lapel. A smoke-colored divider separates the reception area from the grooming area. The reception counter has an attractive display of products for purchase, from shampoos to pet combs, to trial sized specialty foods and treats.

You explain you are new in town, have a new puppy, and simply want to see the facility. The receptionist is courteous, friendly and helpful. You notice someone coming through a door at the rear of the shop. She explains employees have a separate entrance and that is one of the groomers coming in to clip one of their award-winning poodles. She gives an extended tour of the shop and asks if there are any questions. As you leave, she hands you a colorful brochure about the shop and its services, and makes a point of saying she hopes they will be hearing from you soon.

Shop #2 is located on the edge of town on a hobby farm. A large billboard sign with the name "Personal Touch Pet Grooming" carved in country-style lettering is permanently fixed at the end of the long, winding driveway. As you enter the driveway, the paved road splits, with one paved path going to the left, leading to the residence, and the other paved path veering to the right where another sign, similar to the first, is posted. It is lit by ground level floodlights. This sign says, "Personal Touch Pet Grooming – Parking." The parking lot is also paved and well-marked. Down the center of the lot are painted paw prints leading to the shop entrance. The building itself looks like a large playhouse. It is painted white with bright blue accents on the door and window shutters. Matching blue and white striped awnings cover the bay window of the waiting room, the front entrance and a side employee entrance. Upon entering, a bell rings and, in a matter of seconds, the receptionist comes to the counter.

To the left, the waiting area has a small sofa and several upholstered chairs. There is also a tot table with crayons, coloring books and puzzles. The wall on the far right is a chalkboard where waiting children can entertain themselves using the colored chalk provided. An ample supply of individually wrapped towelettes sit on the corner of the reception counter for easy clean up of chalk-dusted hands.

A small TV/VCR unit, accompanied by 15- and 30-minute tapes about animal care and some children's tapes sits on a cart in the corner. The magazine rack houses a range of interests from women's to sports to pets to children's books. A floor-to-ceiling glass-block wall is behind the reception area on the left. To the right is a rest room and display case of pet products.

The receptionist is dressed in a brightly colored smock jacket and has a name tag pinned to the lapel that says, "Janice." You once again explain to the receptionist that you are new in town and have come to see the facility. You also recognize this as the name of the person you spoke with on the phone and mention it to her. She replies, "are you Jezebel's owner?"

After acknowledging you are, she says, "I am so glad you decided to come in to see the shop. Let me show you our facility." She briefly describes the philosophy of the shop as being a family-oriented place and points out the special activities for the children of customers who prefer to wait while their pets are being groomed. Someone enters through the side door and Janice immediately introduces him to you as one of the groomers. "This is Tom. He has been a groomer here for three years and has two cocker spaniels of his own. Tom, Mr. [your name] is looking for a groomer for his new cocker spaniel puppy. You might have the privilege of giving Jezebel her first bath!" Tom responds enthusiastically with, "I can't wait to meet her!"

After the tour, Janice asks, "what other questions can I answer for you?" Once you've asked everything you can think of and prepare to leave, she hands you a trial size packet of doggie treats. The shop's business card is carefully stapled across the top edge. She says, "please give these to Jezebel with our compliments and don't hesitate to call the number on the card if there are any other questions you might have."

Shop #3 is located in a mini strip mall in a residential neighborhood. It is an end shop, with ample parking. The signage is in a bright neon purple and draws attention to the shop. While the sign is colorful and inviting, the first thing you notice is that the brightly lit letters of the shop's name has one burned out letter, so the sign appears to read: Pet als Grooming. The shop window sports a professionally lettered phrase across the top that says, "Welcome to Pet Pals Grooming" please come in."

Inside and to the left, the waiting area has a round coffee table in the corner, with four chairs lined up on either side along each wall. Magazines are fanned out neatly in the center of the table and a thermos of coffee with styrofoam cups, napkins, powdered creamer and sugar packets sit on a tray near the back of the table. A small tented sign says, "Complimentary coffee for our customers, please help yourself."

The newly tiled floor is polished. Walls are freshly painted. And although the counter appears to be as old as the building, it is clean and neat. A desk bell sits squarely in the center of the counter with a tented sign next to it saying, "Please ring bell for service." The bottom of the counter is glass encased and holds an array of products for sale. Each product, neatly arranged, has a small, tented sign stating the price. A larger sign is taped to the top right hand corner of the case, just under the cash register, saying, "ask about our quantity discounts!"

A large bulletin board, divided into two sections, is displayed on the wall. One side is titled, "meet our staff" with individual photographs neatly pinned underneath. A short biography of each person is typed and pinned under each photo. The other side of the bulletin board is titled, "FREE Postings" and is filled with information posted by customers. Announcements are posted of new litters for sale and pets for adoption, either from the humane society or from other customers who may have found stray animals. There were photos of lost and found animals. Pet sitters and dog walkers had pinned up their business cards.

You ring the bell on the reception counter and hear a voice from the back of the shop, "I'll be there in a few minutes! Help yourself to some coffee." In approximately five minutes, a young woman hurriedly comes down the hall from a back room and greets you. In her arms she's carrying a partially wet dog wrapped in a towel. "Hi! I'm sorry to keep you waiting. My receptionist only works mornings and I'm a bit backed up today! What can I do for you?"

Once again you explain you are new in town and are checking out groomers for your new puppy. The woman answers, "Well, I'm glad you stopped in. My name is Kate and I own this shop. I'd be happy to show you the place. Come on in back."

She leads you to the room she was working in. She gently finishes towel drying the shivering dog saying, "There, there Conrad, you're all done with your bath. I'll finish you up in just a few minutes." She places him into a large wire 'holding' cage and turns to you. "This is the actual bathing and grooming room. Right now I'm a one-person shop with a part time receptionist and part time cage caretaker. In the room across the hall I have the other animals that are scheduled for grooming today." She opens the door to show you the inside. Neatly organized cages line the back wall. Each cage has a pillow and a water and food dish. Two of the cages have small dogs waiting their turns. When the two expectant dogs look up toward the doorway, they begin to bark. She says, "Don't worry, Oscar, don't worry, Sasha, I'll come back for each of you very soon."

To you she says, "I try to do each animal while the customer waits, but sometimes it's easier if people can leave them for a few hours and pick them up later. Especially on the days when I am working without a receptionist."

She is enthusiastic about her shop. It is evident she loves animals. It is also evident that—at least today—she is overbooked. As she looks at the clock above the bulletin board, she says, "Yikes! I've got another dog coming in for an appointment in about five minutes! Let me give you this rate card and my business card—it also has my home number on it. Call me anytime with any questions you might have or to make an appointment for your new puppy. Thanks for stopping!"

Three very capable shops (remember, the vet said all three shops would give equal quality of work). One shop does not give better service than the others. One shop does not sell better products than the others. So which shop would you choose? Why?

There is no right or wrong answer.

What I want to impress upon you is that your business is often more than how well you serve customers once they choose to do business with you. Everything connected with promoting your business—your ads, your signage, the words coming out of your employee's mouth—should lead customers towards your business. They, too, are part of your success formula. They, too, must become part of your system for consistency.

Targeting a niche market will not narrow the number of customers you can serve. Targeting a niche market increases your potential for attracting very specific customers to your business and, once there, allows you to present other products and services you have to offer.

Chapter Questions/Exercises:

What business are you in?

Who is your customer?

How do your products and services benefit your customers?

What do you give customers they cannot get from your competitors? If your products and services are the same as your competitors, why do customers do business with you instead of them?

How do you — or should you — capitalize on this differentiation?

When you view your total industry's market, are there customer needs not being met? If so, what are they? How could you incorporate one or more of these needs into your product/service mix?

Chapter 5

How To Bridge the Gap Between Your Current Business and Your Ideal Company

What is your ideal company?

As we look at our businesses from the inside out (working diligently to just get through the day), we sometimes lose sight of what we really had planned for the business to become—and what we had planned for our own lives in relation to the business.

To clearly formulate your ideal company, you have to take a step back—back to the time when the business was a concept rather than a reality. Back to the time when you were thinking about the business from the outside in. Instead of being ingrained in the day-to-day tasks, driven by deadlines, you were looking at it from 'above' and driven by your vision. Financial limitations, deadlines and schedules did not exist. There were only wide, open spaces of possibilities, opportunities and potential.

Whatever your ideal company is, it is important to see it in today's light, not tomorrow's shadow. You must be constantly laying the groundwork for your ideal company within your current business. Your ideal company image can and must be defined. Your ideal company procedures can and must exist. You must incorporate your ideal company values and procedures into today's business. Your current business must act like it already is your ideal company.

Let me demonstrate what I mean by elaborating on the Pet Pals Grooming example from Chapter 4.

Eliminate Barriers — Build Bridges

Kate is a typical entrepreneur. She has an ideal company vision. But she also has a start-up business cash crunch. So instead of planning for the vision, Kate abandoned development of her ideal plan and has chosen to 'make do' with the available resources until she is in a financial position to revamp the business into her ideal company. Unfortunately, by adopting this 'make do' compromise Kate is making it nearly impossible to achieve her ideal company.

It doesn't have to be that way!

Here's how Kate can stay on track for her ideal company success without having to increase her cash flow:

Kate's ideal business

Kate became a pet groomer out of her fondness for animals. Ever since she can remember she has been bringing stray cats and dogs home, caring for and grooming them so somebody would want to adopt them. Because many of the strays had scrapes and scratches from being unprotected outdoors, Kate was careful to use gentle products that would not sting or irritate the skin.

Kate also developed a strong network of acquaintances as she searched for homes for the strays. She volunteered at the humane society, got to know many of the veterinarians, and learned about pet nutrition from sales reps who would drop in at the shelter.

Kate had always dreamed of having a grooming service that catered to strays and adopted pets. She believed by just 'making them prettier' strays had a better chance of being adopted. She also believed grooming was not a luxury, it was a necessity for animal health and well-being.

Kate's current business

Kate went to school to learn how to groom animals. She also became one of the best groomers in an on-site salon at a large pet store. When she noticed a local grooming shop going out of business in her neighborhood, Kate seized the opportunity. She bought the equipment and tools at a substantial discount and picked up the remaining nine months of the lease at a reduced rate.

Kate's current business already has many of the elements of her ideal business. The bulletin board she maintains is a public posting site for lost and found animals, new litters, pet sitting and dog walking services, notices from the humane society promoting pet adoption, and literature about pet nutrition.

The pet shampoos and rinses Kate uses and sells reflect her dedication to exclusively using all-natural, gentle and environmentally-safe products. The pet food she sells is of the highest quality and provides complete, balanced nutrition. And from the way she spoke to her two waiting 'clients' in the back room, it is evident Kate not only considers pets to be part of the owners' families, she considers them as part of her own.

Barrier #1:

Fear of not getting enough clients to sustain business

It's already clear there is a specific type of customer Kate could target which is different from the other two shops in town: the adopted pets, the 'mutts', and the strays that wander into people's lives and become part of the family. The interesting thing to note is that she already has this image, but is not marketing it to her specific audience. Her image exists but is not defined. For fear she will lose business, Kate decides to market her shop as one that 'can do it all' – this is a mistake!

Bridge #1:

Specializing WILL attract more customers.

Kate must start marketing her business as the ideal company. Her ads should clearly define her targeted market. For instance, instead of using the 'we do it all' approach, she could say something like:

Pet Pals Grooming: We handle your pets with loving care and gentle products. We use only natural, environmentally safe products on your precious family pets.

OR

Pet Pals Grooming: Lovable mutts, scraggly strays and shelter adoptees deserve TLC, too! Well-groomed pets make healthy, happy companions.

Once Kate has defined her niche, she must use targeted marketing and information in all promotions. She must use the same type of phrasing she used in her ads on letterhead, brochures, rate cards, etc.

Barrier #2:

Part-time receptionist with little or no training

Kate's immediate cash flow only allows for her to hire a part time receptionist and cage caretaker. The receptionist is putting in the time, but does not have 'sales' ability when talking with customers on the phone. Her manner and tone with callers may be losing Kate business.

Bridge #2:

Training is a key element of image definition

Kate must train her receptionist! Training includes how to answer the phone and how to greet customers who come into the shop. She could develop introductory packages, as the other two shops do, to entice new customers. The receptionist must be trained to encourage people to come to the shop, not just answer their questions!

Barrier #3:

Signage needs repair

Does a neon sign (with a burned out letter) reflect a caring, professional business? To a customer, the burned out letter shows neglect and carelessness.

Bridge #3:

Improve the décor

Kate would not have to spend a lot of money to turn the look of her shop into a scaled down version of her ideal company. If possible she should opt for a different outdoor sign to better reflect her shop's market niche. At the very least, she should get the light fixed.

Inside the shop Kate could:

- Expand the bulletin board area (perhaps use three individual bulletin boards or one 'wall size' board) to really showcase adoption programs, lost and found and other pet services.

- Make nutrition brochures available to customers (the pet food sales reps would be happy to leave a supply of these) and include one with each customer purchase to promote good health.

- Sell an environmentally-safe 'pet kit' made up of various products carried in the shop and packaged together for a special price.

- Display 'before' and 'after' photographs of some of the strays that had been transformed with Kate's TLC grooming services.

Barrier #4:

Lack of marketing to gain the type of clientele Kate wants for her business—the adopted pet.

The only advertising Kate is doing is in the yellow pages and, of course, word of mouth from current customers.

Bridge #4:

Go to the source of the target market!

Kate could have inexpensive discount coupons printed for a 50% discount on a first visit or a free nail clip with every bath, or a free environmentally-safe product sample (that she gets at no cost from sales reps). She could then distribute the coupons to the humane society to give to anyone who adopts a pet. She can also leave the coupons with veterinarian offices to give to new pet owners.

These are just a few of the ways that Kate can start to bridge the gap between her current business and her ideal company. It begins with a plan. The plan must be consistent with the vision of the ideal company. Kate must implement as much of the plan into her current business as possible.

You must do the same.

The only way to successfully attain your ideal company is to implement goals and systems for you and your employees that require you to act like you are the ideal company.

For you to successfully attain the goals of your ideal business, everything in your business must be moving toward them. Where your business is today is a mile marker on the way to your ideal business. Every decision you make for your business needs to be made with your ultimate goal in mind. This ultimate goal becomes the driving force and fuels your actions with passion for what you do.

Chapter Questions/Exercises:

What is your ideal business?

> Describe the building.
> Describe the interior.
> Describe your product/service.
> Describe your ideal customer.
> Describe your ideal employee.
> What are your responsibilities?

What is your current business?

> Describe the building.
> Describe the interior.
> Describe your product/service.
> Describe your current customer.
> Describe your current employee(s).
> What are your responsibilities?

Define your image:

> What do customers buy from you?
>
> Why do they buy from you and not your competitors?
>
> How would your customers describe your business and your services/products? If you don't know, ask them! Is that image consistent with the image of your ideal business?
>
> Do you target a niche market of your industry?
>
> If not, is there a current customer segment that is not being served by your competitors? What are their needs? Can you fill those specific customer needs? How?
>
> If you do target a specific niche market, are you honed into their particular wants? How do you show/tell them you know what they need/want?
>
> Does how your business look reflect your image?
>
> Do your employees reflect your image in what they say and what they do? How could they answer the phone and greet customers differently in order to encourage new business?

What barriers currently exist that prevent you from moving closer to your ideal company?

Are there bridges you can build to connect your current business to your future business? What are they? Be specific. Describe them in detail.

Chapter 6

How Paying Attention to the Details Can Give You Your Ideal Business

"Pay attention to the small things and the big things will take care of themselves."

No doubt you've heard this phrase before, or some version of it. Yet, it is a profound piece of advice every business should incorporate into its business philosophy. In Chapter 3 we examined the importance of consistency. Consistency begins with paying attention to the little things. It is the words you use when you answer the phone. It is the "welcome" and the "thank you" and the "how may I help you?" that make a customer feel like you are there to serve him/her. Every business that pays attention to the little things will reap the rewards of satisfied customers who return again and again.

Coupled with the ideal business image you establish in Chapter 5, attention to detail will seamlessly keep you moving closer to your ideal business. The act of documenting the details will set the stage for a systems-dependent business.

Remember my goals pyramid mentioned in the Preface?

A systems-dependent business =
Repeatable performance =
Consistent results =
A business that can virtually run itself!

With a systems-dependent business the systems run the business, the people run the systems. By setting a systems-dependent business in motion, you will develop a business that works not because of you but without you.

A True Story

A few years ago, my husband and I bought a new car to replace the car I was currently driving. We looked at several comparable cars with similar features, of a similar size and in a comparable price range. We test drove them all. Any one of them would have been a good choice and filled our driving needs. But we bought our car from a particular dealer for one reason. We liked the way we were treated from the moment we stepped into the dealership and on through the buying process.

We were not only buying what the car had to offer, we were buying the positive sales process we experienced – the feeling we had when approached by the dealership's employees. This experience was reinforced with every person at the dealership. It was clear our business was important to them and our satisfaction was their priority.

Here are just some of the things that made a difference in our first impression of the dealership:

The receptionist was clearly visible from every entrance to the showroom so we knew exactly who to approach when we were ready to talk with a sales person. She greeted us with a 'welcome' and 'how may I help you?'

When a salesperson was called to help us, she introduced herself, asked what we were interested in and *listened* to our answer. She showed us the car, talked about options and then asked if we had questions. When we said we'd like some time to talk between ourselves, she again repeated her name and stepped away, telling us to let her know when we were ready for a test drive. And she let us alone!

These are all small things. Yet, these are the things that led us to buying our car from this dealership. And the same courtesy and 'make the customer feel important' attitude came from every person who worked there.

Every dealership wants their customers to have this same experience. Yet, for us, it was clear that only this dealership had the systems in place—and had trained their people to use the systems—to ensure we received this exact experience.

Does this mean only perfection will win customers? No! In fact the day we went to pick up the new car, it was not ready at the time we were told it would be. What did they do? They apologized for the delay and explained why there was a delay. It was near lunch time and the sales person told us they needed about another hour. He then said the company would very much like to buy our lunch to apologize for the inconvenience. We were to go wherever we like and simply return with the receipt. We did just that and were reimbursed upon our return.

Was it an inconvenience? Yes. But the way the sales person handled it—by having a system in place to accommodate the situation—made all of the difference in how we reacted to the delay.

The 'system' didn't end when we drove off in the new car.

- We received a follow up call about a week after we picked up the car to ask how the car was performing.

- We were given customer satisfaction surveys that were turned into corporate headquarters. If the dealership received anything less than an excellent rating from a customer, steps were taken to remedy the problem.

- When I took the car in for service, their computer automatically spit out a record of what had been done in the last visits and what I had called to schedule for this visit.

- As I drove into the service garage, the attendant who checked in my car knew my name and I was told how long the service was expected to take.

- If it were taking longer than had been told to me, the service technician came into the waiting room to explain why and ask if I could wait the additional time needed.

- Again, a few days later, someone called on the phone to ask if we were treated well on this service call and if the car had been properly serviced.

All of these were small details. Yet all of these things — even the delays — were handled in such a way that I, as customer, was kept informed and compensated with courtesy. We were made to FEEL like our business was the most important thing to this dealership. What was the pay off for the dealership?

We purchased another car from this dealership a year later. We also told many of our friends and family members how well we were treated. Two of our friends also bought new cars at this dealership.

When Systems are Compromised, the Business Suffers

Unfortunately, the story doesn't end happily ever after. While the systems themselves continue to be excellent systems, at some point there was an obvious break down in employee training — the people weren't following the system. Consistency was lost.

Here's what happened.

The sale process for our second car, again, went beautifully. The service did not. On our first service appointment we drove into the service garage as usual. We got out of the car and waited. Service people buzzed busily around us with other cars, but there was not even a brief, "Good morning, someone will be with you in just a few moments." There was just chaotic activity.

When someone finally did come to greet us, we received a hurried, "could you move your car forward about 5 feet?" We did. (Previously, a service person would have been able to manage this feat.) He then asked why we were there. We waited while he fumbled with the computer to find our records and confirmed the service we had made an appointment to receive. I had driven separately in case we would have to leave the car for the day. He told us how long it would be and my husband decided to wait for the car. I left.

About two hours later, my husband returned home. "I'm never going back there," he said. Waiting well beyond the length of time the service person told him that the car would be ready, he wandered back into the service garage area and inquired about when his car would be ready. The service person said the shop was really backed up today and they were bringing it in right now. As he pointed in the direction of the service entrance, both he and my husband turned just in time to see the garage door come down onto the back end of our car! Everyone stood around and watched as the door automatically retreated to its open position.

No one in the service area seemed to think this was a big deal. Instead of a quick and honest apology and concern for potential damage, my husband received a sheepish, "whoops, wow, sorry about that! We've got a new kid running cars for us today."

My husband asked for his keys, inspected for damage — there was none — and drove off. We have not taken our cars in to be serviced there again. And it is safe to say that our next new vehicle will not be from this dealership.

Can a large automobile company afford to lose us as customers? Probably. But as the old saying goes, if you have a good experience somewhere, you'll tell three people (we did). If you have a bad experience, you'll tell everyone who will listen (and we do).

This dealership was doing everything right. It had systems in place that gave customers consistent service. It had people in place to properly work those systems. Whatever the cause of the breakdown in implementing those systems during that two-year period (lack of employee training, happy customers but unhappy employees, an owner or manager who did not believe in the value of the system, etc.) could be detrimental to this dealership.

Can you afford not to give your customers consistent products and services every time they come to do business with you?

My point is, just having the systems does not mean things will go smoothly. You must train your employees (and yourself) to use the systems. Repeatable performance will only occur if all of the employees follow the system. Consistent results will only occur with repeatable performance. The systems set up the business to succeed. The people who run the systems carry the action through to achieve the end result. Any breakdown in using the system will compromise the consistent performance your customers rely on.

I am sure the dealership never planned for this type of thing to happen. And, they may very well have gotten back on track. Yet, somewhere there was a breakdown in training and/or communication that has cost them two very loyal customers who were enthusiastic advocates for their products and services.

Prepare for Both Success and Error

When I talk about paying attention to the details, I'm talking about planning for every possible scenario you can think of that could affect your customers. A systems-dependent business plans for perfection and prepares for mistakes. Human error, computer glitches and just plain miscommunications will inevitably happen in your business. Yet, how you handle these mistakes will make the difference between keeping or losing a customer.

If you recall in my story above, the dealership did not have our first new car ready for us to pick it up at the time we were told it would be ready. Instead of simply making us wait and avoiding eye contact, they took action. We were immediately told there was a delay. We received an apology and we received the offer for compensation by buying lunch. There are always options that do not have to be costly. They simply have to attempt to compensate an inconvenience.

Your ideal business must incorporate ideal solutions. Determining what employees must do to make things go right—and what employees must do when things go wrong—should be part of the detailed system you devise for your business. The more you can plan for success and prepare for mistakes, the better your customers will be served. Make the customer's experience—even in the face of a mistake—have a positive outcome.

Pay attention to the details.

Chapter Questions/Exercises:

What procedures do you have in place that are supported by detailed instructions?

How do you train your employees to follow these procedures?

Do these procedures align with the procedures that would exist in your ideal company? If not, how could you revise them to support your ideal company procedures?

When was the last time customer service or satisfaction was compromised?
       What happened?
       Could it have been prevented? If so, how?
       What was done about it?
       Do you still have that customer?
       Could the same problem happen again?
       What details could you outline to help employees handle this situation in the future?

Chapter 7

How To Separate the Owner in You from the Employee in You

Whether you are a one-person business or have 100's of employees, there are many different jobs to be carried out every day. If you answer the phone, you are the receptionist. If you draw up client proposals, you are the estimator. If you sell merchandise in your shop, you are the sales person, the clerk and the stock person.

For you to develop a system that will give your customers consistent products and/or services, every single 'job' you or someone else does must be defined.

In Chapter 5 you defined your ideal business. We also talked about the importance of acting like you already are that ideal company. Your business must be prepared to constantly be moving toward your ideal company. It does not matter if only one or two people are currently performing all of the job duties for your business. You must:

- Focus on your ideal business
- Determine the different jobs or positions that exist for the ideal company

- Prepare an organization chart for the ideal company
- Write job descriptions for each position of your ideal company

The Organization Chart

Contrary to some people's beliefs, the organization chart is not designed to show 'who is more important' in the company. An organization chart defines accountability. Accountability is as important to small companies as it is to large and/or growing companies.

Employees must know who can authorize action. Who will be accountable for decisions made on behalf of the company?

The organization chart sets the stage for consistency.

The Job Description & Responsibility Outline

Job descriptions that include a responsibility outline are necessary to prevent chaos. It doesn't matter how small your company is, employees must know what they will be held responsible for in the jobs you are asking them to perform.

Developing job descriptions is even more important if all of the jobs are currently held by YOU!

You must separate your responsibilities as owner from those you currently perform as manager. You must separate your responsibilities as sales manager from those you perform as a sales person. You must prepare job descriptions for every position you envision for your ideal company. You cannot successfully hire someone to take on a set of responsibilities if you have not defined what those responsibilities are. You cannot gradually advance yourself into the owner position if you do not have that position defined!

Chapter Questions/Exercises:

Using your ideal company definition, develop an organization/ accountability chart. A sample is included for you to reference on the following page.

1. List the job positions of your ideal company
2. Decide accountability status
3. Place connecting lines to indicate reporting status

For every position you have shown on your organization chart for your ideal company, develop a detailed job description and responsibility outline. A sample job description follows the sample organization chart.

Sample Organization Chart

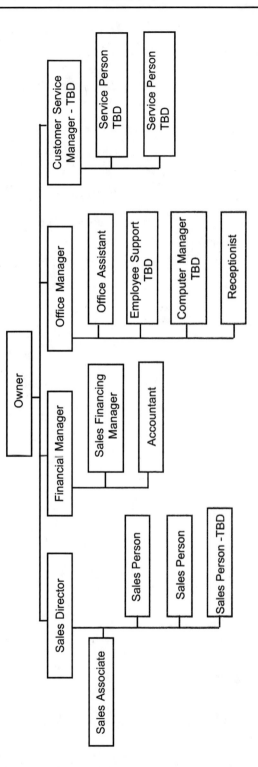

Sample Job Description/ Responsibility Outline
(Retail: pet food supply store)

Job Description for: Salesperson

Reports to: Sales Manager

Overview:

As a salesperson in our store you will be expected to provide customers with assistance selecting products that best meet their pets nutritional needs. You will also be responsible for maintaining the appearance of shelves and displays. We will provide thorough training to familiarize you with our business operations and procedures as they relate to your job and responsibilities.

Responsibilities:

• Become thoroughly familiar with the store's merchandise and learn as much as possible about nutritional comparisons to make informed recommendations to customers.

• Learn the sales process in accordance with our operations procedures to perform at maximum efficiency.

• Work productively while in the store. If there are no customers, maintain the appearance of the shelves and displays.

• Recognize the importance of our customers and show respect for their business by being courteous, professional and available.

• We consider all employees to be team members. Show respect for co-workers by assisting staff members when needed.

• Maintain a professional personal appearance to make a positive impression on our customers.

• Price and stock merchandise when it arrives and build promotional displays.

• Inform management of any customer problems or situations you feel we should be aware of.

Chapter Notes & Ideas

Chapter 8

How To Promote Yourself to the Position of Owner Even If You Are the BEST Employee You Have!

D o you own your business or do you own your job?

Many entrepreneurs find it difficult to not only make the *transition from* having a job to owning a business, but to make the *distinction between* having a job and owning a business.

Remember Paul Planworthy in Chapter 2? He started a business because he knew he could do the work. He did the work. He did it well. He did it so well, and hung on to it so closely that he nearly succeeded himself right out of business! Paul did not own a business. Paul owned his job.

As his business began to grow, Paul continued to do all of the work himself until there were simply no more hours left in the day for him to work alone and meet deadlines. Even when Paul hired Biff, he was not hiring an employee, he was hiring a co-worker. Paul continued to put in his eight-hour shifts on the shop floor. Who was looking out for the future of the business?

Yes, if you want something done right, you *can* do it yourself. However, if you want something done right and you want to be the business owner, you must *train others* to do it your 'right' way.

If you really want to own a business, not a job, eventually you have to let go of the daily work to concentrate on the business itself. How can you successfully train others? Let me introduce you to the master/apprentice approach to training.

The Master/Apprentice Approach

In the master/apprentice approach to training, you are the master. Employees are your apprentices. You must teach your apprentices how to do things YOUR way.

Many of you may groan and say, "Susan, I TRIED to show employees how to do what I do, but they just don't care like I do, and even if they care, they just don't 'get' it."

I believe you believe this statement is true. But I'll tell you why I don't necessarily believe apathy or ineptness is always the employee's fault. Sometimes it is the owner who is setting employees up to fail.

How long did it take you to learn your craft? Whether it is running machinery, making a product, fixing someone's car or giving business advice, your special, unique talent or skill is something you developed over time. Most likely you started out as someone else's 'apprentice.' Someone else taught you how to do what you do so well. You must do the same for your employees.

What are the jobs only you can do? Perhaps you are a carpenter with skills you learned by shadowing your grandfather. Perhaps you are a baker who has 'just the right touch' with French pastries. Or perhaps you are the 'whiz kid' of advertising. You can come up with just the right headline, campaign theme or brochure copy that gets your customers instant recognition and results. All of these capabilities are indispensable to the success of your business. Yet all of these things have a process that ensure the right outcome.

If you are a carpenter who learned how to do things 'right' from your grandfather, you learned in a slow methodical way. You learned by doing, failing, and doing again and again. You were your grandfather's apprentice.

If you are a baker, you didn't 'stumble' across the right combination of ingredients to make your specialty pastries. There is a process. Perhaps you learned it, or perhaps you developed it through experimentation. Regardless of how you came by this expertise, or how long it took to perfect, it did not just suddenly appear.

The same is true for the advertising "whiz kid." There is a thought process and an ability to expand your imagination that seems to be instinctive in the way you come up with ideas. Yet, your so-called instinct is based on fundamental knowledge and understanding of the advertising world (and game). That 'instinct' comes out of a methodology of creative enhancement. Those methods can be shared. They can be learned by others.

The point I must make here is that everything that makes you valuable can be passed on to others and make them valuable, too. The key is to:

1.   Develop specific procedures

2.   Spend the time to properly train others in those procedures

3.   Reinforce the necessity of consistency of those procedures to your employees so they are always serving the customers as you would serve them yourself.

Remember the goals pyramid:

> **A systems-dependent business =**
> **Repeatable performance =**
> **Consistent results =**
> **A business that can virtually run itself!**

You are the one who must demonstrate the repeatable performance of your systems-dependent business in order to achieve consistent results. If you are not a great master, you will not cultivate great apprentices.

There is a 'right way' for every employee action and reaction. It is your responsibility as owner — the one with the vision — to determine what the 'right way' is that best serves your business, and impart that ability to others.

Every job in your business, from the receptionist's position to the president's position, is a craft that must be carefully and purposefully taught to fully realize your ideal business concept.

Develop specific steps for every job responsibility. Let employees know the importance of each and every step. Let them witness your own dedication to doing it well and doing it right. You are the master. Let them see how what they do is important to the overall business and how it impacts every other aspect of the business. Gradually, you will confidently advance yourself from the day-to-day involvement as employee to the all-important job for business survival as owner.

The steps you develop are the procedures for your ideal company. These procedures will lead to consistent, predictable results. And when you have procedures in place that can achieve consistent, predictable results, then your business can and will run without you.

Chapter Questions/Exercises:

Using the job descriptions and responsibility outlines you developed in Chapter 7, develop detailed procedures for each specific job. Begin with the bottom of the organization chart and work your way up the accountability ladder.

Keeping your ideal company in mind, answer this question:

How would *you* do this job?

- Write down the steps and procedures to accomplish each task associated with the job.

- Make it a learnable procedure by using the words, "step one, step two, etc."

- Be as detailed as possible.

- For every action, ask yourself why you are doing it this way. Write it down.

If a job is difficult to describe on paper, outline the training stages needed to teach an apprentice how to properly learn the job.

For instance, if you are a restaurant owner who is training a new wait staff person you may decide that:

- For the first day or two, the apprentice should simply follow you around to watch, observe, and ask questions.

- The second day or two, begin to involve the apprentice in the first step of the procedure. Demonstrate what to do. Then, have the employee demonstrate it back to you.

- During slow times at the restaurant have other wait staff pose as customers. Comment and correct (in a positive manner).

Continue this process until the apprentice has 'mastered' the first step, then go on to the next.

Whatever procedure you decide to use to train a new apprentice, write it down! There will come a day when you will be training the trainers. It is necessary to provide documentation so those trainers can properly train new apprentices to do it YOUR way.

Chapter 9

How To Get Your Employees to Support Your Business Success System

The truth is you can't *make* an employee do anything. Sure, you can threaten, you can impose consequences, you can withhold pay or penalize, but none of these tactics will force an employee to support your business system. And none of these things will make them better employees or more interested in helping your business to succeed. Employees work for you because there is something 'in it' for them to do so.

Many years ago when I was in advertising we called it the WIIFM — What's In It For Me — factor. At that time we were focused on determining reasons for potential customers to buy a product or service sold by our clients. By answering WIIFM from the customer's viewpoint, we were better able to hone in on the benefits of a product or service — the selling points necessary to convince people to buy. If there is no benefit, there is no incentive to hand over their hard-earned money.

The WIIFM factor is appropriate when looking at employees, too. As the owner, you know what's in it for you — a business that will help you to reach your personal and professional goals. Yet to encourage employees to adopt your business operations system and support your business, you must also determine what's in it for them.

What do you think is the top motivator of employee performance? It may surprise some of you that it is not money. According to a recent survey by the Council of Communication Management, the top motivator for employee performance is recognition for a job well done. Money definitely has its place, but it does not in and of itself give employees job satisfaction. Therefore, when hiring new employees, or in trying to determine how you can motivate current employees, it is important to find out what they need from you to increase job satisfaction. It is also important to be realistic about what you have to offer.

Why Hiring the Inexperienced Can Work to Your Advantage

The master/apprentice approach to employee training I talk about in Chapter 8 is ideal for use with inexperienced employees. Whenever possible, hire the inexperienced. Why?

Inexperienced employees:
- Are eager to learn.
- Want an opportunity to gain the experience they lack.
- Have no preconceived ideas of how a business should run.
- Are free of pre-learned habits.
- Are more cost-effective for your growing business.
- Will be most willing to accept your business system. They will LEARN IT AND DO IT YOUR WAY.

For a systems-based business, inexperience is not a hindrance to excellent performance. In fact, you may see a marked improvement in performance because employees will know exactly what you expect from them.

When Hiring the Inexperienced Isn't Possible

While I advocate hiring the inexperienced whenever possible, there may be times when it is necessary to hire someone with experience. For instance, an auto repair shop needs mechanics. Experience, or at least technical training, is required. At these times, keep the following in mind:

1. Be realistic about what you have to offer an experienced new hire. Don't make promises for benefits or incentives that you know you can't meet.
2. Clarify your expectations for the position. This includes your expectation for new employees to learn, understand, be trained in and follow the company's operating procedures.
3. Be sure to ask potential candidates what their goals are. If you can't deliver on advancement opportunities, reconsider hiring someone whose priority is to quickly advance to another position.
4. Ask candidates what they particularly liked and disliked about a previous job. It will give you insight into whether or not the same conflicts could arise as an employee in your own business.
5. Listen to your instincts. 90% of the time they will be right on the mark!

How to Get Current Employees to Change Their Habits

Many of you will already have employees who work for you. As you devise your business system, it is likely you will be asking these employees to change some of their work habits to align with the new, more efficient system. Inevitably, you will get resistance.

Employees who have already been trained, will not want to be retrained. They will often resent new policies and procedures introduced into the business after they've already worked there a length of time. You will hear, "I already know how to do that," or "I like the old way better," or worse yet, you won't even hear the complaints, you will simply discover they continue to do it the 'old way' whenever they can get away with it.

This behavior undermines your authority, creates discord in the business and will eventually become a problem if you want your new business system to succeed. Why should other employees do it your way if you don't care that some of the employees are doing it their own way? How can you get current employees to change with the business?

I refer you to the WIIFM factor mentioned at the beginning of this chapter. Attach a benefit to learning the new system. Incentive programs don't have to be expensive. Recognition and reward for a job well done is a positive way to reinforce progress in learning the system. Find the benefit for employees to invest their time and talent into learning new ways to perform old tasks.

1. <u>Begin with an employee survey</u>. The more you know about what motivates your employees, the better you will be able to encourage them to adapt to the changes you are about to implement. Never assume you know what your employees want. Ask them.

2. <u>Explain why you're changing things</u>. From the feedback I've received from clients who have implemented a new business operations system, explaining to current employees why you are making changes is always helpful. No one likes to simply be told what to do. Explain the importance of the system to the continued success of the business. Explain the importance of the system to consistently serve the customer. Explain that, once the system is implemented, it will make each of their jobs easier because it will take the guesswork out of handling difficult situations.

3. <u>Identify the direct and indirect benefits employees receive by working the system</u>. "Do it or you'll lose your job" is not an incentive! If possible, tie in a reward for performance (see Addendum I "5 Creative Motivators to Turn Apathetic Employees Into Superstars"). Change the rewards and the programs when necessary. Maybe you'll need one kind of incentive to encourage people to learn the system. After three months, you may find it beneficial to switch to a different type of incentive. For instance, motivator #2 is to "Catch Employees Doing Things Right" — you may want to use this incentive at the onset while employees are beginning to implement new procedures. After three months, you may want to switch to a

team incentive so employees begin working together and apply the new procedures for a group reward.

4. <u>Use a reward system that includes ALL of the employees, not just your managers</u>. The people who do the day-to-day work

deserve to be recognized as much—*or more*—than your management staff.

Chapter Questions/Exercises:

Using the job descriptions and responsibility outlines you developed in Chapter 7, develop an 'ideal employee' profile for each position. What characteristics would be most desirable for each specific job? Use this profile when you interview for new employees.

Develop an employee survey to help determine the WIIFM factor of your staff. What kinds of incentives are they most likely to work for? Refer to Addendum I for some ideas on possible motivators.

SECTION II:

The Business of Doing Business

Chapter 10

Why You Must Document Your Operating Procedures

If you have answered the questions and performed the exercises in Section I of this book, you have invested a lot of time to view your business with a new perspective. You have begun the process for building your systems-based business. Don't stop now! You've got to pull it all together into a usable operations manual. This step is key to attaining consistent results from your system.

Think of it this way...

Construction people don't build houses without blueprints. Chefs don't create award-winning entrees without recipes. Football teams don't win games without game plans. Why do businesses expect to succeed without their version of a blueprint, recipe, or game plan?

Let's use the game of football as an example. Every player on a football team has a specific job. Each one learns the job by practicing the plays associated with his specific position on the team. A player doesn't just read the game plan and automatically know what to do on game day. A player practices over and over again to perfect the moves — master the game. The more a player practices the plays, the more consistent he becomes. The more consistent a player becomes, the more valuable he is to the team. And when all of the players are performing consistently, the chances for success of that team increase.

A good, solid, consistent game plan wins games. A good, solid, consistent operations manual increases your chances for business success.

Once again, I refer you to my simple goal pyramid. It applies to winning football teams as well as to successful businesses:

> **A systems-dependent business**
> (the game plan of a football team) =
>
> **Repeatable performance**
> (players practicing the specific plays designed to win the game) =
>
> **Consistent results**
> (players instinctively knowing what to do when game day arrives) =
>
> **A business that virtually runs itself**
> (the coach is on the sidelines calling the plays, not throwing the passes or tackling the opposing team's quarterback)

Specific plays of the game (operations procedures) must be documented. The game plan (operations manual) must be used.

To win in anything you do:

> *You've got to plan the work and work the plan.*

This is why you must document your operating procedures.

Bigger Isn't Always Better: How Big Should An Operations Manual Be?

There were times when my clients thought they could only get their money's worth if the manual was the biggest and heaviest one I'd ever written. But bigger doesn't always mean better and it is much more difficult to write text in a clear, concise way than to simply ramble and ultimately say very little. Who wants to sift through pages and pages of useless text?

The size of your operations manual will be determined by the size and type of business you're in. The more facets (or divisions, products or services) there are to your business, the more information will need to be included. Some businesses like to include supplemental material as separate sections of the manual. This might include a detailed advertising plan that has been developed by an agency. It may include manuals for equipment used in the business. It may include the latest month-end financials for the business. As long as the operations procedures of the business remain in tact and are not *replaced* by these items, the manual is a good place to keep all of these things together.

In the following chapters I'll be giving you detailed instructions on how to organize your information into an operations manual. If you focus on its potential value as your business' individual game plan, you will walk away with a clear, concise set of procedures that will help you achieve the consistent results needed for current and future success.

Chapter Notes & Ideas

Chapter 11

Sample TOC

On the following pages is a general outline for a Table of Contents (TOC) which demonstrates the type of information used in a typical manual. Use this outline as a reference as we begin the process of organizing your specific manual contents.

Operations Manual

Preface
>A Letter from the President/Owner
>Our Corporate Philosophy

The Industry
>Industry Overview
>Market Position

The Organization
>Company History
>Future Outlook
>Business Description
>Facilities Description
>Product/Service Mix
>Market/Customer Mix
>Employee Names and Numbers

Business Management
>Daily Reports
>Weekly Reports
>Monthly Reports
>Quarterly Analysis
>Annual Operations
>Cash Drawer Procedures
>Accounts Payable
>Chart of Accounts
>Insurance
>Payroll

Daily Operating Procedures
>Opening Procedures
>Closing Procedures
>Store Appearance Standards
>Daily Reports
>Scheduling
>Daily Duties Checklist
>Supply List
>Loss Prevention
>Bank Deposit Procedures
>Charge Card Acceptance Policy
>Check Acceptance Procedures
>NSF (non-sufficient funds) Procedures

Security Procedures
> Security Systems
> Security Measures
> Security Policies and Procedures

Emergency Procedures
> Emergency Procedures
> In the Event of Robbery
> In the Event of Burglary, Theft, or Vandalism

Salesmanship and Selling
> Principles of Effective Salesmanship
> Qualifying the Customer
> Identifying the Key Decision Maker
> Using Key Benefits Statements
> Overcoming the Obstacles
> Presenting the Close
> Sales Style
> Basic Telephone Techniques
> Listening Techniques
> Sales Vocabulary

Sales Policies and Procedures
> Market Prospecting
> Sales Follow-up
> Sales Reports
> Anatomy of a Customer Order
> Order Form/Receipt
> Order Processing
> Invoice

Customer Service
> Product Knowledge
> Returns/Exchanges
> Special Orders
> Handling Complaints / Angry Customers

Advertising and Promotion
> Market Planning
> Market Analysis
> Customer Analysis
> Budgeting for Marketing
> Media Analysis
> Metropolitan Newspapers
> Television
> Trade Publications and Magazines

Direct Mail
Outdoor Advertising
Radio
Competition Analysis
Budgeting Advertising Expenditures
Advertising Planning
Public Relations and Publicity
Camera-Ready Artwork and Ad Mattes
Letterhead, Envelopes, and Business Cards

Merchandising
Display
Product Placement / Floor Plan
Pricing
Signage

Inventory Management
Approved Product Specifications
Opening Inventory
Inventory Control
Inventory Planning
Product Pricing
Sales and Markdowns
Stock Carryovers
Warehousing

Computer Systems Operations
Introduction
Overview of Software Function

Personnel Administration
Job Descriptions
Methods of Recruitment
Application
Interviewing Techniques
Selecting and Hiring Employees
Compensation
Vacation and Time Off
Insurance
Employee Discounts and Incentives
Employee Dress and Appearance Standards
Equal Opportunity Employment Policy
Discrimination Policies
Employee Probationary Period
Performance Review System

Chapter 12

Organizing the Process

To prepare for the process of documentation, you've got to organize the information into specific category headings. As you can see from the sample Table of Contents in the previous chapter, you will be putting together a lot of information.

As many different ways as I have tried to implement a more sophisticated system of information gathering, I continually go back to the one I describe in this chapter. It has always been the simplest way for me to organize contents for an operations manual. Use it as a guideline and modify it to fit your own preference for organization. (See the diagram at the end of this chapter for a visual description of the process.)

Supplies

- <u>An empty file drawer or a cardboard banker's box</u>. Keep all of your operations manual materials and information together and separate from your day-to-day paperwork.

- <u>A box of file folders</u>. A separate folder will be used to hold the information and procedures for each specific task outlined in the manual.

- A box of 10" x 13" clasp envelopes or accordion style folders. These will be labeled with general section (or category) headings (i.e., Daily Operations, Customer Service, etc.). You will be placing completed file folders for individual tasks into the appropriate section-titled envelope.

- Various sized sticky-backed notes and a highlighter. The notes come in handy to make quick notations that can be attached to information as you begin to separate it into specific file folders. The highlighter can be used to emphasize important points or portions of information that need revision.

- A tape recorder (optional) and word processor. After separating information into file folders, you will review each folder's contents and may need to create, elaborate on or revise the current information.

- A three-ring binder with a clear plastic insert sleeve on the cover (the binder spine should be 1-1/2 or 2" capacity). This will hold your first draft and final operations manual pages.

- Index dividers. Use a divider to separate (and label) each category heading when placed in the binder.

- Three-hole punch. It's the only way to get your pages into your work-in-progress manual!

Gather Current Information

You may be surprised to discover how much information you already have for your manual.

- Gather together any and all forms that are used in your current business, whether routinely or on rare occasions. Don't concern yourself with separating the information into folders. The initial goal is to simply get a copy of everything in one place (the banker's box or file drawer).

- If you have instructions for the forms, make sure you acquire copies of those as well. You may have a handful of job descriptions, invoices, purchase order forms, an employee manual, safety rules, and government required postings. If you have a business plan, include a copy of that in the information.

- Any contracts or agreements you use with your employees, your vendors, your customers, or your contractors should be included in this information.

- Ask your supervisors and employees to compile their own set of procedures. They may also be willing to document procedures that have no written form or instruction but exist simply because 'someone told me it was done this way.'

- Print out copies of all the exercises you performed in Section I of this book.

At this gathering stage, do not concern yourself with the validity or necessity of each item or procedure. If it is currently being used somewhere in your business operations, put it in the pile. It is likely you will be shocked at how much paperwork—and sometimes duplication of work—you will discover. If you begin to see a pattern of duplication, ignore that at this time. The evaluation of the information comes later, after we've gone through several other steps.

Once you've amassed as much information as you can, you're ready to begin separating information into categories and individual folders.

Organization Process

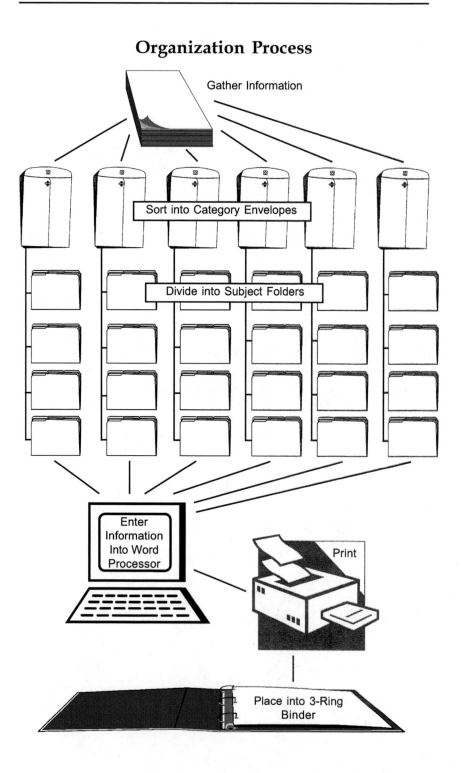

Gather Information

Sort into Category Envelopes

Divide into Subject Folders

Enter Information Into Word Processor

Print

Place into 3-Ring Binder

Chapter 13

Setting Up Your Manual Sections and Subjects

Before you begin to separate the stack of information you gathered in Chapter 12, you want some semblance of how the different pieces of information will be organized. Begin by using the clasp envelopes (or accordion files) and labeling them into these general categories (from the sample Table of Contents in Chapter 11):

Preface
The Industry
The Organization
Business Management
Daily Operating Procedures
Security Procedures
Emergency Procedures
Salesmanship and Selling
Sales Policies and Procedures
Customer Service
Advertising and Promotion
Merchandising
Inventory Management
Computer Systems Operations
Personnel Administration
Other

What Goes Into Each Category

Use these general guidelines for separating your material and placing it into specific category envelopes. Don't allow yourself to get bogged down trying to determine exactly where a piece of information must go. Use your first instinct. You can always change its placement later when we take each category individually and begin to evaluate the information.

As you begin to separate information into these general topics, an entirely new topic that is unique to your business may surface. Do not try to place it into a category where it does not fit! By all means, feel free to make a new category (and envelope) or temporarily place it into the "Other" category.

Preface

The preface serves as an introduction to the company. If you have a company philosophy or mission statement, perhaps from your business plan, place it in this category. This would also be an excellent place to include your vision of the ideal company developed in Section I.

The Industry

This section should include an industry overview and any history and statistics about its growth, technological evolution and projected future. Also include a description of your market position within the industry.

The Organization

Include information you have about the company's history and a description of your business, both in terms of the customers you service and the facility itself. Include a copy of the floor plan if you have one. Information and lists of the products you sell or the services you provide should also go in this category. Use the target market information and organization chart you developed in Section I. Also include an employee listing of contact names and phone numbers.

Business Management

The Business Management section includes the policies and procedures used for managing the business. Any reports that you generate on a daily, weekly, monthly, quarterly and annual basis should be described here along with procedures for report preparation and presentation. Your accounting practicing and payroll procedures can also be included in this section. You might also want to include procedures for maintaining confidentiality and security of this information.

Daily Operating Procedures

Details of your office or store appearance standards and procedures for daily tasks and operations belong in this category. Use information you developed to define task responsibilities for job descriptions, and appropriate master/apprentice training procedures from the Section I exercises. Include opening and closing procedures, and daily tasks such as employee scheduling, check and charge card acceptance, bank deposits, gift certificates and shoplifting/theft deterrents (loss prevention). Include procedures for items that are taken out in the morning and put away at night and procedures for cashing out the registers at the end of the business day.

Security Procedures

Security is important to protect your business and your employees. Use this section for policies and procedures for using your security system or describe the security measures taken by your building's landlord.

Emergency Procedures

Include procedures for every potential emergency, including fire, theft, burglary, vandalism, and medical.

Salesmanship and Selling

This section should include everything you use to help your employees do a better job of selling your products and/or services. Incorporate the information you developed in Section I using the master/apprentice approach to training for jobs related to sales. Procedures should be consistent with a sales style that best reflects the company image. Address subjects such as telephone scripts, industry terminology, overcoming objections, and principles of effective selling for your type of service or product.

Sales Policies and Procedures

Your sales staff must understand the procedures of the paperwork for a sale as it goes through the office for processing. Include procedures you have in place for required sales reports, customer order forms or purchase orders, invoices and delivery.

Customer Service

It is important for customers to receive excellent customer service from you and your employees. All policies and procedures that support customer service should be in this category including requirements for product knowledge, procedures for handling customer complaints, returns or exchanges and special orders.

Advertising and Promotion

Based on your type of business and scope of customer demographics, advertising may include local, regional or national (or international) advertising and promotion efforts. Include your advertising plan, budget, and copies of the ads you have used or intend to use in your promotions.

Merchandising

If you have a retail business, include your policies and procedures for product displays, pricing, and signage. Also include your floor plan and shelving layout.

Inventory Management

Keeping track of your inventory is critical to preventing loss, spoilage or waste. Don't throw profits out the window because you haven't kept track of inventory. Include your specific procedures for inventory planning, control, pricing, and conditions for markdowns and sales. Document your warehouse layout so you can easily accept deliveries, pick products and pack deliveries.

Computer Systems Operations

Computer systems can be simple or elaborately networked together to automatically track transactions from sales to accounting and maintain communications with vendors, customers and other employees. Your manual should include an introduction to how your particular system is designed to work, and an overview of software functions that employees must be trained on to properly learn and use the system.

Personnel Administration

The personnel section is often the largest category of information in a manual. Many business owners develop portions of this section into a separate employee manual. Therefore, you may want to divide this into two subcategories.

Administration would include job descriptions, methods of recruitment, interviewing techniques and selection, hiring procedures and advice on what you can and cannot ask during an interview to prevent any discrimination claims, performance review system and forms for warnings or termination.

Employee policies and procedures would include compensation, vacation, holidays and time off, dress and appearance standards, discounts and incentives offered by the company, and a description of the performance review system.

Other

Review the remaining information in your stack of gathered materials that did not fit into the general category headings. Most likely this will be information specific to your own industry or market segment. Create as many new category envelopes as necessary to place all of the information.

Once you have gathered and placed all the forms and operational information you have into these general category listings, you are ready to individually review the contents of each envelope and develop the first draft of your manual.

Chapter Notes & Ideas

Chapter 14

Preparing Your Manual's First Draft

Using your box of file folders and a tape recorder or word processor, you will begin the documentation procedures for your first draft of the operations manual. (Refer to the diagram at the end of Chapter 12, page 102.)

The following steps are to be completed for each individual category envelope that you created in the previous chapter. Do only one envelope at a time.

Separate Contents of Each Envelope

1.   Choose a category envelope (or accordion file).

2.   Separate the contents of the envelope into specific subjects and place each subject into a file folder. For instance, in the Daily Operations category envelope, you will have included information for opening and closing procedures, daily reports, check acceptance, gift certificate procedures, etc. Each of these subjects is to be placed into a separate file folder and labeled accordingly.

3.   Include all information, procedures and forms that currently exist for each subject.

Review Contents of Each Folder

1.   For each subject folder, remove the existing information.

2.   Review the information for:
   a. Consistency with your ideal company vision
   b. Completeness of step-by-step procedures to properly perform the task
   c. Forms, checklists or paperwork that do or should accompany the task to be performed

3.   Review and, if necessary, revise the procedure instructions (and corresponding form) to include detailed descriptions that will answer the following: Who, What, When, Where, and How (see step 4)? Use the tape recorder or access the word processing file containing the existing procedure and make your revisions directly into the computer file.

4.   For example, for the folder labeled gift certificates, review and revise the information to answer the following:
   a. **Who** is responsible for filling out, approving, and processing the certificate?
   b. **What** should be done with the paperwork immediately upon issuing a certificate?
   c. **When** does the certificate get entered into the system?
   d. **Where** are certificates stored for employee access?
   e. **How** is a certificate given to the customer? Is there a special envelope used?

In fact, there are two sets of procedures to describe here. One for issuing a certificate (above), and one for redeeming a certificate. Both should be included in this folder.

For example:

   a. **Who** is authorized to accept a certificate being redeemed by a customer?
   b. **What** is done to redeem the certificate? Is there a special key on the register to indicate payment by certificate? Must it be initialed by the receiving clerk?

    c. **When** is the transaction complete? Upon entry into the register or are there other steps for completion?

    d. **Where** is the certificate placed once it is redeemed? In the cash register as cash or a check would be? In a separate drawer or box?

    e. **How** is the certificate processed? Does the procedure get passed on to the accounting function? Is it counted with receipts at day end by the clerk?

Note: My clients often challenge the need to be so detailed and specific when stepping through procedures. After all, some of the instructions (like answering the phone or taking a phone message) are very simplistic. Although some of these procedures may seem more like common sense, everyone's idea of 'common' is not the same.

Ultimately, you are the one to decide how detailed each procedure description will be. Your goal is to attain consistent behavior by each and every employee, which, in turn, provides a consistent expectation of service to the customer. Remember the success achieved by McDonalds? Stay focused on the success you want to achieve for your ideal company. Both hinge on the ability to create consistency of the smallest detail.

5.   When you have finished with the contents of one file folder:

    a. If you are tape recording revisions, simply go on to the next file folder;

    b. If you are entering revisions directly into a word processing program, print out the pages, three-hole punch them <u>and put them into the file folder</u> with a copy of the corresponding form (if there is one).

6.   When you have finished all of the file folders for one category envelope, put all of the file folders back into the envelope, and move on to the next category envelope.

7.   Follow these steps for all of the category envelopes and file folders.

8.   Separate the information from your miscellaneous or "Other" category envelope into file folders. Follow the steps outlined above to document the procedures. Determine if new category headings should be created to accommodate a grouping of file folders, or if these file folders can be incorporated into one of the existing category headings. Create new categories as needed.

9.   If you have been using a tape recorder to develop your procedures, have the information on the tape transcribed into a word processing program, with each file folder subject saved as a separate computer file. Print out each file subject, three-hole punch the pages, and place them into the corresponding file folder.

Sort, Organize and Place Pages Into the Binder

Using the dividers, label tabs for each category heading (the headings assigned to the envelopes). Behind each category tab place the three-hole punched information from the subject file folders of the appropriate category envelope. If there is a corresponding form for a subject, make a copy of the form, three-hole punch it and place it with the procedure.

Continue with each divider and contents until all pages are placed into the three ring binder.

Chapter 15

How To Streamline Your Business to Squeeze More Profits from Your Current Business

If you have worked your way to this page, then you have successfully completed the first draft of your operations manual. You've covered a lot of ground!

With your first draft in hand, this is an excellent time to analyze functionality, purpose and efficiency of your operations. Whether you have made many changes, or very few, to how you view and operate your business, this chapter will help to focus on increasing productivity, eliminating redundancy, and reducing errors—all of which contribute to bigger profits and more time for you!

Streamlining your business is all about identifying—and fixing—the three biggest profit eaters of your business:

1. The paper trail.
2. The people trail.
3. The technology trail.

The paper trail.

The simple act of physically following a piece of paper through the office can be an eye-opening experience. Here's an example of how one of my client businesses used to handle a phone inquiry:

Initiation: Someone calls in to receive information about the company.

Action 1:   Receptionist writes information onto 'Information Request" form.

Action 2:   Receptionist makes a copy of the form.

Action 3:   Receptionist forwards the original to the sales department and files the copy in a follow-up 'tickler' file for 5 days after request was received.

Action 4:   Sales secretary receives form and assigns sales person for response.

Action 5:   Sales person writes personalized cover letter and assembles literature requested, gives to secretary to package and send.

Action 6:   Secretary creates label, packages information into an envelope, places postage on envelope, and puts into outbox for mailing.

Action 7:   The form is marked "processed" with the date and the name of the assigned sales person. A copy is made for that sales person's follow up file and the original is sent back to the receptionist to verify the date info was sent.

Action 8:   Receptionist pulls the form from the tickler files, discards it and files the processed form in a chronological file in case the caller should call to inquire about his/her inquiry.

Action 9:   At the end of each day, the receptionist pulls out the forms that have been filed for 5 days but have not come back processed. A second copy is made of each one and forwarded to the sales secretary as a reminder with the stamp "2nd notice" stamped on the front.

Action 10:   Another round of the same process begins.

This is NOT an efficient way to serve customers!

In following this one piece of paper through the company, how much time has been wasted; how much unnecessary handling did this request receive?

To some of you, this whole scenario may seem ridiculous and redundant. Let me assure you it happens in thousands of companies every single day. And it happens because "it's always been done this way" in those companies.

The people trail.

Following the people trail is more difficult than following the paper trail. Unfortunately, it sometimes takes a customer complaint to initiate investigation into a people problem. Could something like this happen at your company:

With every intention of setting next year's advertising budget you arrive at work, pour your first cup of coffee and pull out all of the reference material and financials from last year's campaign. At 9 a.m. there's a knock on your office door. The receptionist has a customer on the phone wanting to know when he can expect to see the back ordered items he's been waiting for—they have been back ordered for two weeks. You take the call, knowing you can immediately access the information on your computer.

While you check the order tracking, you pick up the phone to exchange pleasantries with the customer. He is not interested in conversation; he wants to know about his order. He has never had to wait for two weeks for any of the items, which were usually in stock, and his business will suffer if he cannot take delivery soon.

Unfortunately, the computer tracking system shows no special order or follow up for this customer. Without disclosing the fury you begin to foster for this error, you calmly say to the customer that your computer records do not show a delivery date, but you will surely look into the matter personally and call him back with a definite date.

It's 9:15 a.m. and the advertising budget will have to wait.

The customer did mention he placed the order with your best sales associate — Bob. You go to the sales floor to find him. Bob is currently helping a customer so you wait for him to finish before approaching him.

At 9:45 a.m. Bob begins to ring up the purchases of his current customer on the register. As you wait, you notice Bob re-keys the entries three times. Bob knows you are waiting to speak with him so he enlists the help of another sales person on the floor to finish ringing up the sale. Bob thanks the customer, invites her back for the big sale beginning next Wednesday and presents here with a free gift with purchase coupon she can use at that time.

You ask Bob to join you in the break room so you can talk privately. You describe the conversation you had earlier with the unhappy customer, who is eager for delivery of his merchandise. Bob remembers taking the order and acknowledges there was a problem when he submitted it via computer. "So I just gave the order over the phone," says Bob. "It should have been here more than a week ago."

It is now 10:15 a.m. and you are on your way to the shipping and receiving area. The 10 a.m. delivery truck from your distributor in Chicago is still being unloaded. While you wait for the receiving manager to complete the check in, you strike up a conversation with Gina, the order entry person. When you mention you are tracking down an order Bob had placed by phone rather than through the computer system, Gina replies sarcastically, "What a surprise." As you question Gina about her reaction, you discover that Bob is notorious for bypassing the computer system. He places orders verbally and sometimes presents a handwritten note with the order information which he then asks her to enter into the computer. Most of the time Bob simply comes back to shipping when the customer arrives to get an order. The paperwork is processed after the merchandise has already arrived.

When presenting Gina with the order in question, she recalls such an order did arrive last week. However, since it was not recorded in the computer as a special order for a specific customer, the items were placed into inventory and shelved in the store.

The truck is finally unloaded by 10:45 a.m. and Lenny, the manager, is quick to verify Gina's description of how Bob handles special orders. "Yeah, he just can't get the hang of using the computer," says Lenny.

You return to the retail floor, searching for the items the customer had special ordered. Sure enough, they had been shelved. Luckily, they had not been resold. You take them off the shelf, go to the register and ask a sales person to ring up the sale as fulfillment of a special order. Of course, when entered, it comes up as unpaid since there is no corresponding order entry for the prepaid special order. You tell the sales person you noticed he helped Bob out earlier to ring up a sale. "Yes," she says, "Bob has computer-phobia, so we all try to help him out whenever we can."

You take the incorrect receipt, bag the merchandise and head to accounting. Explaining the situation, you ask the accounts person to adjust the entries as needed to balance the books.

Back in your office, you call the customer and tell him you have tracked down the order, it has indeed arrived and, as an apology for the inconvenience, you will deliver the merchandise to him personally. He has been a long-standing, high-ticket customer and you cannot afford to strain this relationship. Since it is nearly 11:30, you ask if you can take the customer to lunch when you drop off the merchandise. He accepts.

It is nearly 2 p.m. when you return to the office from your delivery and lunch with the customer. You have a board of directors meeting starting at 2:30 and it will take the rest of the day. No problem, the advertising budget can wait until tomorrow.

So there was a glitch in operations today. These things happen. It all turned out fine and all it cost was a customer lunch you were happy to oblige anyway. You easily justify today's events because:

Bob is your BEST sales person. He brings in more repeat business than anyone in the store. The customers love being served by him and his co-workers rally around him. He comes in early and he stays late whenever he's asked. He's great with setting up creative and interesting displays and he always gives 110%. You do not want to lose Bob as an employee. His computer phobia is his only flaw and it isn't going to hurt a thing to let Bob rely on others to help him with the computer.

Whether Bob is your best employee or not, there are real costs associated with today's events:

1.   The CUSTOMER has been waiting for an order well over a week after its delivery to inventory. That costs HIM money and compromises his confidence in your company's ability to deliver what he needs.

2.   The sales associate who rings up Bob's sales is taken AWAY from her job of generating her own sales from customers currently browsing the store. If it takes two people to service one customer, another customer may walk out of the store without a purchase he/she may have made if a sales associate were available. That costs YOU money in potential sales.

3.   You spent from 9 a.m. until 2 p.m. tracking down the problem and 'putting out the fire' from one incident. What is *your* time worth to the company?

4.   The small amounts of time spent talking with Lenny, Gina, the sales associate and accounting personnel take them away from whatever they are doing at the time. To "fix" the problem Bob set in motion has made those around him less efficient which also costs the company money.

5.   You are not getting the value you paid for out of your computer system if ALL employees do not know how and learn how to properly use the system. That costs you BIG money.

How much value are you really getting from your operations system if Bob is excluded from having to learn the same processes and procedures expected from the other sales associates?

How will you handle the Bob situation?

1.   Leave things the way they are. You're willing to allow the inefficiencies caused by Bob's ineptness with computers. They are no big deal.

2.   Retrain Bob on the computer system. Do it with patience, understanding, and persistence. Explain how learning the system benefits Bob.

3.   Restructure the sales department to fit with Bob's abilities. Change responsibilities so the sales associates only do the selling. Have separate cashiers ring up the merchandise. If Bob never has to use the cash register, he will never make an error that could cost the company a customer.

Special exceptions for any employee can be costly and damaging to your business. Remember that in the business operations success formula, <u>systems run the business</u> and <u>people run the systems</u>.

The technology trail.

Normally I do not consider technology to be a profit-eater for businesses. However, improper use of technology can be a huge expense—rather than a smart investment—for a small business. Here's one way I've seen technology become a profit-eater:

A few years ago one of my clients proudly announced the company (a nutrition supplement retail store) recently computerized its business and operations. To my horror I discovered the company's new computerization was adding to its INEFFICIENCIES rather than relieving them of it. Why?

Although the company had indeed put a computer system in place, it lacked the ability to automate paperwork from the front of the house (customer transactions) to the back of the house (accounting). So, even though employees were entering data into computer files, they continued to process the paperwork in the same manner they used prior to implementing the computer system!

My initial reaction was that whomever the business owner relied on for computing advice had grossly under-performed as a reputable consultant.

However, as we continued with our operations evaluation process, it eventually became clear that the client himself was very scattered in articulating what he wanted to accomplish by installing a computer system. The consultant may not have asked all of the right questions, but the client also wasn't clear about what he needed—or even what he was currently doing. This was a clear sign to me that the client was not only inconsistent in what he did in his business, he was also not analyzing how work was being processed through the business.

Paperwork is one of the largest efficiency-stealers of every business. Computerization is THE answer to remedy 99% of the bottlenecks, yet business owners do not objectively analyze what they are doing prior to trying to implement computers into the operation. To just have the technology is not enough. Specific objectives need to be defined so best use of the technology results in increased efficiency and greater productivity.

Let's look at how technology could resolve both the problems previously identified in the paper trail and the people trail.

The paper trail

Initiation: Someone calls in to receive information about the company.

Action 1:   The receptionist enters the caller's information directly into a contact database on the computer.

Action 2:   At the end of the day, the receptionist merges the list of new requests with a template for a cover letter, and labels, prints them out, packages letters and literature and mails the information. The sales department is automatically sent via computer a copy of the day's transactions for inquiry requests.

Action 3:   The sales department is reminded by the computer after 5 days to follow up on those requests.

The original 10 action steps have been pared down to 3. This saves time, trims costs, and reduces the potential for problems due to miscommunication or employee error.

The people trail

If both Bob and the receptionist were properly trained on the computer the error would never have occurred. If a customer did call to check on an order status, ideally the receptionist would handle the phone call! With access to the computer tracking system, which is already in place, and trained how to properly use it, she would have been able to take the call, check the back order, and inform the customer of its status. The call would have come in at 9 a.m. and she would have been through with the SATISFIED customer by 9:05 a.m.

You would have been uninterrupted to finish your ad budget, and Bob would be happily serving customers on the sales floor.

Steps for Streamlining Your Operations

• Review the information placed in each category of your manual. Consider the potential impact of these three profit-eaters on your own business as you assess each procedure:

The paper trail: how can you improve the flow of paperwork through the office? As you review specific procedures written in your first draft, do some of them duplicate other procedures? Do some of the steps of the procedure seem to be redundant? Determine how many times a form is handled from its initiation to its conclusion. Are there ways to reduce or eliminate some of those steps?

The people trail: how can you improve the efficiencies of your employees? Are employees ignoring or making exception to some of your established procedures? If so, find out why. Determine if those reasons are valid. If they are, consider changing the procedure. If they are not, take steps to retrain and explain the value — both to the company and to the employee — of performing the established procedures.

The technology trail: have you incorporated technology into your business? How has the use of technology improved your operations? If it has not improved operations, find out why. Do you fully understand its capabilities? Are employees learning how to properly use it to do their jobs better, faster and more accurately? What processes or procedures have been replaced by the use of technology? If your computer system is viewed as an expense that costs you money instead of an investment that makes you money, you are missing the value of incorporating technology into your business. Contact your computer consultant to discuss how to make your system a real asset to your business.

- As you review the entire first draft, use sticky-backed notes to flag pages that need additional thought or revision for maximum procedure effectiveness. Always ask yourself: *how will what is done at this level best serve the customer?* This is your absolute bottom line.

- After you have gone through the entire manual enter the new revisions into the existing computer files to update the procedure. Print and three-hole punch the revised pages and replace the existing pages of the manual with the new ones.

- It is not uncommon to go through this revision process two or three times before finalizing the information. When you believe you have reached your final draft, ask someone else to read through the information and provide feedback. Make additional revisions based on this feedback.

Chapter 16

Putting It All Together:
Your Final Operations Manual

You have spent a lot of time to develop your business success formula and document procedures to achieve consistent performance. The final step is to make it easy to access information and easy to update the manual as needed.

1.   Cover sheet for the three-ring binder

In the list of suggested supplies for your manual, the three-ring binder came with a clear protective sleeve on the front cover. Prepare a page that includes the following information:

[Your company logo (optional)]
[YOUR COMPANY]
Operations Manual
Copyright [date]

These pages can be as simple or as graphic-intensive as you want. Most people include their company logo. Others don't bother. This is an internal document (unless you are planning to franchise) so spend more time on perfecting the content, not the cover!

If you do not have a clear sleeve on the cover, use this page as the first page, before the Table of Contents.

2.   Typefaces

Use easy to read typefaces for the text of your manual. Script, decorative and Old English styles are not recommended. Stick with the classics. There's a good reason they are used time and again for manuscripts. Here is a list of the most common typefaces:

> Times Roman
> Bookman
> Palatino (this book uses Palatino)
> Helvetica
> Garamond
> New Century Schoolbook

Use bold, italic and underlining to emphasize specific points in your text, but don't overdo it. Avoid using ALL CAPITAL LETTERS! While they may provide emphasis, they make information difficult to read, are more distracting to the reader and have a connotation of SCREAMING AT THE READER instead of emphasizing a point.

Use bullets and numbered steps when describing procedures.

3.   Page numbering

Before you print out a final copy of your manual, you need to give some thought to page numbering. Using a standard sequential numbering system, from 1 to 999, is difficult to update without resorting to unusual tactics if you add pages. For example, if you add two pages after page 17, you would have to number those two pages 17a and 17b in order to maintain the sequence for page 18.

A better choice is to number pages within each section. In a word processing program, this is very easy to do. Simply save all of the chapters of one section in one electronic file. Use your word processor's numbering capability and designate a section number and page. For instance, the pages of your first category would read, "Page I-1, I-2, I-3, etc. The pages of the second category would be II-1, II-2, II-3, etc. See sample Table of Contents with page numbers at the end of this chapter.

Any updates within chapters of a single section are easily updated and result in reprinting the single section rather than the entire manual.

4.   Layout

Over the years I have had clients who want elaborately designed layouts for their manuals. They use clip art and photos and various other graphic elements for headers and footers. You are certainly welcome to do the same. However, fancy page layouts do not improve the content of the manual! I prefer a clean, simple look to each page. A simple page layout example is included at the end of this chapter.

5.   Additional Information

Depending on your specific business, it may be useful to include a final section to your manual with additional information. For some, it might be a Frequently Asked Questions & Answers section. Many companies like to include instructions for equipment use that come from the manufacturer. The purpose of this manual is to make everything in your business serve the customer by informing and educating the employee. Give them all the tools they need to make your company look great!

Sample Table of Contents—Page Numbering System

Operations Manual

V-10   Charge Card Acceptance Policy
V-11   Check Acceptance Procedures
V-12   NSF (non-sufficient funds) Procedures

Security Procedures
VI-1   Security Systems
VI-2   Security Measures
VI-3   Security Policies and Procedures

Emergency Procedures
VII-1   Emergency Procedures
VII-2   In the Event of Robbery
VII-3   In the Event of Burglary, Theft, or Vandalism

Salesmanship and Selling
VIII-1   Principles of Effective Salesmanship
VIII-2   Qualifying the Customer
VIII-3   Identifying the Key Decision Maker
VIII-4   Using Key Benefits Statements
VIII-5   Overcoming the Obstacles
VIII-6   Presenting the Close
VIII-7   Sales Style
VIII-8   Basic Telephone Techniques
VIII-9   Listening Techniques
VIII-10 Sales Vocabulary

Sales Policies and Procedures
IX-1   Market Prospecting
IX-2   Sales Follow-up
IX-3   Sales Reports
IX-4   Anatomy of a Customer Order
IX-5   Order Form/Receipt
IX-6   Order Processing
IX-7   Invoice

Customer Service
X-1   Product Knowledge
X-2   Returns/Exchanges
X-3   Special Orders
X-4   Handling Complaints / Angry Customers

Advertising and Promotion
XI-1   Market Planning
XI-2   Market Analysis
XI-3   Customer Analysis

Sample Cover Sheet

Pet Pals Grooming

**Confidential
Operations Manual**

Copyright 1999

Sample Category Title Page

SECTION III

Daily Operating Procedures

Opening Procedures
Closing Procedures
Store Appearance Standards
Daily Reports
Scheduling
Daily Duties Checklist
Supply List
Loss Prevention
Bank Deposit Procedures
Charge Card Acceptance Policy
Check Acceptance Procedures
NSF Procedures

Sample Procedure Pages

Opening Procedures

Opening of the shop is the responsibility of the owner or a member of the store management team that includes the store manager, assistant manager or shift supervisor. Opening procedures are:

1. Disarm alarm system. Always be aware of the environment around you as you open the door and disarm the system. If you notice anything suspicious, contact the local police immediately.

2. Turn on approximately 50% of the lighting in the store. The remaining light fixtures should not be turned on until opening to avoid giving the store an "open for business" impression to customers.

3. Boot up the office computer terminal (instructions are in Computer Section XIV).

4. Verify that all Daily Reports have been run for the previous night. If they have not been run, do them at this time. Also check the previous night's checklist to verify that the backup was completed.

5. Balance the cash drawer(s). We recommend a cash mix of:
   $ 20.00 One twenty dollar bill
   $ 20.00 Two ten dollar bills
   $ 55.00 Eleven five dollar bills
   $ 37.00 Thirty-seven one dollar bills
   $ 10.00 In quarters
   $ 5.50 In dimes
   $ 2.00 In nickels
   $ .50 In pennies
   _____
   $150.00 Total amount in cash drawer(s)

6. Prepare the daily deposit for the bank if it has not been prepared from the previous evening.
   A. Sort coupons, checks, and credit card receipts
   B. Run daily credit card batch reports
   C. Balance shift totals to report
   D. Balance total day's revenues and coupons to cash drawer summary for all stations
   E. Prepare bank deposit ticket
   F. Complete weekly deposit report

7.   Conduct a check of prior night's closing duties checklist. Duties that have not been completed should be done at this time, prior to opening for the day's business.

8.   Log in to work stations at the counter area. Check:
• receipt paper
• credit card paper
• register ribbon

9.   If hazardous conditions exist in the parking lot due to weather, salt and clean the area as needed for the safety of employees and customers. Periodically check during the day to keep areas clear and safe.

10.   When the opening hour arrives, turn on the remaining lights and unlock store for business.

CLOSING PROCEDURES

Closing procedures are to be performed each evening to prepare for the following day, and to ensure security when the building is empty. The procedures are:

1. Check the entire shop to make sure all customers have left the building. Remember to check the back room areas and restrooms.

2. Turn off the lights in the front section of the shop.

3. Shut down computer. TURN OFF MONITOR. Take cash drawer summary.

4. Remove cash from register(s), take it to a secure place, and count each drawer back to the beginning balance of $150.00. Balance to cash drawer count sheets.

4. Closeout reports that need to be run from the computer where report printer is stationed.

5. Confirm completion of duties on Daily Cleaning Schedule (refer to Store Appearance Standards on the following page of this manual.)

6. Place the money in the safe. Lock the safe and recheck to make sure it is locked.

7. Turn off the remaining lights in the building.

8. Set the alarm before exiting the building. Observe the areas outside the shop and in the parking lot to be sure it is safe to leave the building. If you have any concerns, contact local police.

9. Double check doors prior to leaving. Make sure they are locked.

STORE APPEARANCE STANDARDS

The shop's first impression is critical to properly build a reputation and positive relationship with customers that encourage them to be comfortable, loyal and pleased to be a life long member of the **Pet Pals** family.

Housekeeping responsibilities must include both the interior and exterior of the building. The following list of expectations is to be monitored on a daily and /or weekly basis. Schedule maintenance recommendations as outlined.

Shop Front
1.   Front windows.
The front windows of the shop should be cleaned professionally a minimum of once a month, both interior and exterior. We recommend the outside windows be cleaned once every two weeks.

2.   Sidewalk and parking area.
Sweep the front sidewalk area as needed, or at a minimum of once every week to ensure that the front sidewalk is swept and clutter-free for customers. This area must also be kept clean from snow and ice during the winter months.

3.   Clutter.
Get rid of it! A consumer's first view of our business is through the windows of the store. Make sure there is no clutter or dirt visible from outside or inside the store. Do not allow bulletins to be posted in the store windows. Invite people to use the in-store bulletin board for posting notices (approved by management). To conserve space, only pet-related notices are allowed to be posted.

4.   Signage.
Make sure that the outside signage is appropriately lighted and clean. Also check the parking lot lighting for dim or burned out lights. Report the need for replacement lighting to the property management landlord.

Retail Store Area
1.   Front counter(s).
The front counter area fills up all too quickly with clutter. It is imperative to make it a daily duty to keep this area clean and presentable. To maximize the working space, keep it organized and clutter-free. Sweep and clean around this area frequently during the day, since the counter and floors become dusty and strewn with particles from the bulk products being handled.

Keep unnecessary supplies stored in the back room—there are very few supplies that must be stored in the counter area.

Clean the counter top(s) daily with cleaning solution. Make sure to include the area under and around computer terminal. The computer system must be kept free from dust and dirt to ensure proper working order. Take extra care when cleaning around the computer system to avoid damage.

2.   Floors.

Daily: The floors should be swept daily using a dust mop. We recommend that this be done each night after closing.

Weekly: Tile floors will need to be buffed a minimum of once each month.

Every six months: Floors should be stripped and waxed every six months, and should be contracted with a professional cleaning floor service.

3.   Pet accidents.
Occasionally a customer's pet will have an "accident" in the store. Clean it up immediately! Both disinfectant and deodorizer must be used.

4.   Lighting.
Panels need to be cleaned regularly and all fixtures should remain clean and in good working order. Replace bulbs as needed.

5.   Food rotation & presentation.
All food products must be rotated for freshness. This should become a standard procedure when receiving new product.

Face product to the front of shelf on a daily basis and clear any dust or particles around the product shelving. Front facing product presents well and eliminates the need for additional depth of product on the shelves.

6.   Non-retail areas.
All back rooms and office space, warehouse areas and restrooms should be cleaned a minimum of once per week. If not well maintained, these areas can become hazardous and must remain clean and organized, regardless of their "behind the scenes" location.

7.   Fixturing.
Dust fixtures a minimum of once per week. Clean fixtures of any scuff marks as needed with a liquid cleaner.

Daily Reports

Daily

At the close of each business day run the Close the Store from the Master Systems Menu. You can select several different report options from store station maintenance. You can choose from the following options:

• Daily transaction tax audit report.

• Daily transaction summary by transaction number and time.

• Daily transaction summary by payment method.

• Daily summary by register station.

• Daily Summary by Salesperson.

• Combined totals for all cash drawers.

• Daily sales by Department / Category / Item.

• Daily summary of ledger postings.

• Lay Away Report (If lay-aways are posted during the day).

SCHEDULING

Prepare worksheet for schedules a week in advance and post schedules seven days in advance (minimum) of the next work period.

Breaks are scheduled as follows:

- one hour unpaid break for every eight hours worked

- 30 minutes unpaid break if an employee works less than 8 hours, but more than five

- a ten minute rest period for every four hours worked

Customer service is our priority and we must staff accordingly. Determine schedules according to the number of customer appointments and determine high traffic times for adequate staffing.

General business hours are from 10 a.m. to 7 p.m., Monday-Saturday. Sunday store hours are 1-5 p.m.

SUPPLY LIST

The following is a list of supplies needed for daily shop operations.

Category I: Cleaning

1) Trash bags
2) Trash cans
3) Paper towels
4) Windex/409/Dow
5) Hand soap/dish soap
6) Towels
7) Brooms/mops/dust pan
8) Toilet paper
9) Feather duster
10) Detergent
11) Fabric softener

Category II: Store

1) Pens
2) Staples/stapler
3) Calculator
4) Tape measure
5) Scissors
6) Tape

Category III: First Aids

1) Band aids
2) Peroxide
3) Neosporin
4) Gauze

Chapter Notes & Ideas

Chapter 17

Should You Consider
Franchising Your Business?

Now that you've taken the time and invested the analytical energy to put your business in the profit zone, what next?

What is your ultimate goal for your business? Do you want to grow into a larger single-site company? Do you envision opening multiple locations locally, regionally or nationally? Do you want to take your business to a level of success that will make it an attractive purchase to someone else, thus freeing you to retire or start something completely new?

Depending on your answer to "what's next?" it is not at all unfeasible that you might want to grow your business by turning it into a franchise.

Here are some of the franchising basics:

Franchising is a method of distributing products or expanding operations. Every business basically has four expansion alternatives:
(1) pursue vertical markets,
(2) diversify
(3) acquire or merge with another company, or
(4) franchise.

Vertical marketing is based on the invention of new applications for existing products. Diversification is accomplished by introducing new products or entering new industries. As a growth strategy, franchising provides a business with the ability to rapidly enter new markets by increasing the number of distribution channels or outlets. Franchising also permits a company to diversify its sources of income by generating franchise fees and royalties.

Successful franchise businesses have a unique or competitive product associated with a protected trademark. The business format must be well documented and easily replicated, so it can be transferred to others. A typical franchise system has a training program for franchisees, architectural plans and product specifications, operating procedures, management controls, and assistance with purchasing, inventory, marketing, and advertising.

Here is the International Franchise Association definition of a franchise:

> A franchise is a continuing relationship between franchisor and franchisee in which the sum total of the franchisor's knowledge, image, success, manufacturing, and marketing techniques are supplied to the franchisee for a consideration.

> The franchisee pays a financial consideration to the franchisor and invests the money required to start the business. The franchisor supplies an optimized business system or exclusive product, a recognizable identity, and know-how. The franchisee must usually abide by the franchisor's quality standards and product specifications, yet, despite this relationship, a franchisor and a franchisee are not legal business partners. The franchisee is the exclusive owner of the business.

> In many cases, purchasing a franchise means acquiring a prepackaged business. However, although the franchisee owns all the assets, the franchisor may have a strong voice in how the business is run. The cornerstone of every franchise is a contract that defines the rights and obligations of the franchisor and the franchisee.

A typical business format franchise includes:

Licensed Trademark

The franchisee receives the right to use the franchisor's trademark, name, logo, or other commercial symbol, thus taking advantage of the parent company's reputation and image.

Training Program

The franchisee receives training in operating the franchise business. Franchise training programs can range from two days to six months depending on the complexity of the business. Training usually includes:
* industry background
* site development
* accounting, purchasing, and inventory methods
* product preparation, manufacturing, or merchandising
* sales and marketing
* advertising and promotion
* staff hiring and training
* technical or industry-specific training as necessary

Operations Manual

The franchisor's trade secrets, know-how, and experience are documented in a confidential operations manual loaned to franchisees for the term of the franchise. A good manual includes detailed policies, procedures, and techniques for starting and developing the outlet, ordering initial supplies and inventory pricing and merchandising, preparing or selling products, outlet management, hiring and training staff, personnel policies, bookkeeping techniques, and technical aspects of the business.

Specifications, Blueprints, and Layout Designs

Franchisors often provide specifications and designs for building and operating the outlet to unify the visual identity for architecture, construction, fixtures and signs. Franchisors may also provide approved supplier lists, opening inventory lists, and detailed specifications for equipment.

Advertising Systems

Many franchisors administer a cooperative advertising fund. Franchisees contribute a small percentage of their outlets' gross revenues to this fund. This pool is generally used to finance major national or regional campaigns to benefit all franchisee outlets.

Franchisors may also assist individual outlet owners through the preparation of standard advertising materials, such as fliers, commercials, or camera-ready artwork for newspaper or magazine advertisements. Most franchise agreements force franchisees to abide by their franchisors' advertising standards and to use only artwork and language approved by the franchisors' advertising departments.

Ongoing Assistance

A typical business format franchise includes provisions for ongoing assistance, such as on-site troubleshooting and guidance by a field manager or consultant.

If you are interested in learning more about franchising your business, contact:

International Franchise Association
1350 New York Ave., Suite 900
Washington, DC 20005

Parting Words

Stick with the Game Plan to Master Your Operations

No how-to book in and of itself will make your business a success. Not even the highest paid business consultant in the country can do that. Only you can choose to apply proposed principles and strategies to your own business.

In these pages, I have outlined the basic elements necessary for you to put your business game plan together. Hopefully, I've helped you to look at your business from a more focused perspective in terms of identifying goals and attaining them by detailing your actions and procedures to support those goals.

As we finish our work together, I want to once again remind you of the goal pyramid I introduced in the Preface and refer to throughout the text:

A systems-dependent business =
Repeatable performance =
Consistent results =
A business that can virtually run itself.

If you have completed the exercises in Section I and documented your operations procedures as outlined in Section II, you have your game plan in hand for a systems-dependent business.

Practice it. Support it. Master it.

Unleash the strategies you have developed to build repeatable performance by your employees and begin the process for consistent result.

Remember that your business does not own you. You own your business. With the right tools, the best procedures and supportive employees, you achieve and maintain control. You hold all the power to make your business run without you.

As a final note, I encourage you to send me your success stories and your business challenges. At the beginning of this book, I told you the writing of it was the direct result of clients who expressed common, specific needs. I now consider you a client, too. My job continues to be to find ways to help you make your business run smoothly and become more profitable.

I can only do that with your feedback. What about this book helped you the most in your specific business? What information would you like to see expanded upon? What other areas of business do you struggle with and cannot find the resources to help solve your problems?

I invite you to contact me via email with your comments and suggestions. We can all do a better job if we learn from the experiences of others.

To your success . . .

Susan Carter
E-mail: susancarter@successideas.com

P.S.   For more business-building advice and information, visit my Web site at: **www.successideas.com** You'll find useful (and FREE!) articles, book chapters, and ezines.

Addendums

Addendum I:
5 Creative Employee Motivators

Addendum II:
Financial Aid Resource Guide

Addendum I

5 Creative Employee Motivators

How To Hire — and KEEP Superstar Employees

Introduction

Whether you are hiring new employees or trying to motivate those who have been with your company a while, the biggest asset you will have in your business is PEOPLE. They represent you and your business. They set the tone with new customers. And their interaction with those customers is primarily responsible for repeat business (and increased — or decreased — profits for you!).

What management task is more important than finding a good person for a job with your company and knowing how to keep that person satisfied?

Improve Your Hiring Tactics

Before you can successfully motivate employees, you've got to hire the ones who best fit what you and your company need. While this seems a bit elementary, many of my clients over the years have admitted that they dislike the hiring process. They claim it is too time-consuming and, based on some of the employees they've hired, consider the selection process to be as accurate as a roll of the dice in Las Vegas!

As I've demonstrated throughout the text of this book, the value you can expect to receive is dependent on the effort you're willing to expend. The hiring process should be one of the most effort-intensive actions you perform. After all, you are seeking people to represent you to your customers.

Here are a few ways to make sure you get what you want, and want what you get:

1. If you know what you're looking for, you have a better chance of finding it.

If you are unclear about the duties and responsibilities related to the position you are hiring for, then you are already sabotaging your efforts. It amazes me how many interviewers know what the job title is for a position, but have only a vague idea of what that person will be doing.

Every coach of every successful sports team knows exactly what every position on the team requires from its 'superstar' players and so should you. Before you begin your search for a new employee, be clear on the specific skills and/or knowledge that person must have to successfully perform in the position. Develop a 'profile' of your ideal employee. Ask yourself these questions and BE VERY SPECIFIC with your answers:

- What are the tasks / responsibilities of this position?
- What skills must an employee have to perform them?
- What personality traits are needed to best perform them?
- What opportunities exist beyond this position that might be attractive to a potential employee?

Write down the answers and refer to them before each interview. If you are clear about what you need, the interview will go better, and it will be easier to determine what each applicant has to offer to fit your 'superstar' profile.

2. If you plan to mine for gold, you've got to sift through a lot of rocks.

When you're looking for a new employee, how many applicants do you interview? Do you try to keep it down to 5 or 10? If you're looking for a superstar, you've got to at least double those numbers! Many owners/managers interview far too few people. They view the interviewing process as something they just 'want to get through' as quickly as possible to get to the end result ('hire someone') instead of keeping an eye on the goal ('hire a superstar').

Whether you're looking for a sales person, a receptionist, a stock person, or a vice president, stay focused on the goal. Hiring an employee in haste because the pressure is on to fill a spot, could become the costliest mistake you will ever make.

3. If you're going to win the game, you've got to keep score.

Okay, so you've developed the profile of your ideal employee. You have decided to talk to at least 20 people. You have arranged 5 interviews a day for 4 days. That's a lot of people in a short amount of time. After the first 3-4, it's easy for confusion to set in. You need a way of keeping track of your impressions of each applicant.

Create and use a checklist listing the skills and personality traits of your 'ideal' employee for the particular position. Immediately after an applicant leaves the interview, 'score' the person according to your ideal criteria with a '10' being perfect. Then write in anything additional that particularly impressed you or surprised you, including your 'gut' instinct about the person.

These checklists will help you to narrow your choices for more in-depth interviews with a select few. And don't forget the 80/20 rule: the interviewer should speak only 20% of the time and listen 80% of the time.

4. *If you want a diverse response, you've got to use diverse tactics.*

If you need an employee with specific skills, you need to find creative ways to recruit him/her. For instance, let's say you run an automotive service shop and you need a skilled mechanic. Put the ad in the paper, yes. But don't sit back waiting for a line to form outside your door. Be proactive. Post an ad at the technical schools, place small ads in newsletters of motoring clubs, offer a finder's fee to your mechanics who can recommend someone that ends up signing on. Let people who work for vendors and suppliers know that you are looking; ask if they know anyone who might be interested.

Also, give a potential employee a reason to want to choose YOU over the other people looking for similar employees. Know—and communicate—the benefits of working for you. For instance, which sales job ad do you think drew more responses:

Ad #1:

> Salesperson needed for pet store. Prefer some retail selling experience. Helpful if you know about animals. Must be willing to work nights and weekends. Advancement opportunities. Call between 10 and 12 to set an interview appointment.

Ad #2:

> Love pets? We want YOU! Excellent sales opportunity for energetic animal lover who likes working with people. We offer an on-the-job training program, rapid advancement possibilities, flexible hours and a merchandising discount. Work in a modern pet store with a great group of people. Call for an interview.

You'll attract more superstar applicants if you promote the job offer in a beneficial way. Make them want to work for you!

5. *View the job from the other side of the desk.*

For you to get the employee you want, and for the employee to get the job he/she wants, there has to be a benefit for both of you.

When interviewing to determine skills, attitude and characteristics that you seek from an applicant, don't forget to also solicit feedback about what that person wants from YOU. A paycheck, sure. That's understood. But employees seek other benefits, too. The more you can determine what motivates this person to work, the better you will be able to motivate that person to want to work for YOU.

Remember that employees don't have two separate lives: professional and personal. The two are intertwined and the goals they have are based on the two working together. You won't be able to totally figure out what an employee's goals are, but there are a few questions you can ask that might help you determine if what the job you are offering will satisfy the applicant, and if the applicant can satisfy the job.

Here are a few questions that may help you gain insight into a potential employee's goals and characteristics:

1. Tell me about your last job. What aspects of the job did you like best? What did you like least?

2. Why do you want to work here? What attracted you to our ad?

3. What problems would you have if we asked you to work weekends, evenings or rotating schedules?

4. What would your dream job be?

5. Part of our hiring policy is to phone past employers. When we call yours, what will they tell us about your work?

Let applicants know that you are interested in their satisfaction with the job. Ask them to rank the following in order of importance:

Help with personal problems	_____
Interesting work	_____
High wages	_____
Job security	_____
Personal loyalty of supervisor	_____
Tactful discipline	_____
Full appreciation of work done	_____
Feeling of belonging	_____
Good working conditions	_____
Promotion in the company	_____
A company to be proud of	_____
Pleasant coworkers	_____
Traditional benefits (health, etc.)	_____
Flexible work schedule	_____

There are no right or wrong answers. Yet how potential employees rank these desires will give you insight into how well you can provide them with what they value based on your knowledge of your own business and how work gets done.

By putting time and effort into finding employees who will enhance your business, you will save time, effort and MONEY by having to replace those who do not get what they need from you or — worse — employees who stay but are no longer assets to your business.

Two, Four, Six, Eight — What's the Trick to Motivate!?

You've worked hard to find and choose superstar employees. Now how do you get them to perform? As discussed earlier in this book, you can't *make* employees do anything. And that's why it is important to try to predetermine what people value before you hire them. Someone who is very interested in opportunities to climb the corporate ladder will soon be bored and disillusioned if there is no foreseeable chance to realize that opportunity. Yet, while you cannot make people do what you need them to do, it is possible to encourage people to do what you want by offering incentives.

Incentives have proven to be a great motivator and they do not have to be expensive. There are various no-risk programs that can be set up based on profits so it is a win-win for all of you.

While individual incentives are an excellent way to encourage people to do their best, I also recommend setting up team incentive programs that get your people working together — towards the same goals. Also keep in mind that different age groups are motivated by different incentives. Some like cash, some like time off, some like luxury certificates for things they might not normally buy themselves like dinner at a four-star restaurant and a limousine ride and theatre tickets to the hottest show in town. The best way to find out what motivates your employees is to ask them! Remember: if you make a program fun and challenging — with attainable rewards — your employees benefit, you benefit, and so do your customers.

Choosing Incentive Rewards

Make sure employees acknowledge that the rewards are worth the effort. Let them know what the 'prizes' are at the same time you announce the program. Be sure employees are enthused about them, not cynical! And, if you have 'team programs' make certain the reward can be equally split or shared, or that each winner receives the same reward.

Avoid incentives requiring additional employee investment. Don't just give a free dinner at the city's most expensive restaurant. Is that employee really going to dine alone? Always make it dinner for two or a night on the town for two, or a weekend for two, etc. If you want employees to really be excited about your incentive program, the reward has to be given with 'no strings attached.'

Here are a few suggestions to get you thinking about appropriateness of rewards:

<u>Store shopping spree</u>.

If you are a retail business and the merchandise you sell is something your employees would like having themselves, the prize could be a storewide shopping spree of any item or group of items that have a retail value of $100 (or whatever amount you choose). Obviously, if your business does not sell products employees would enjoy personally (like office supplies) or you already offer significant store discounts to all employees, this may not be an appropriate incentive.

<u>Time off with pay</u>.

Just like kids in school, free days are popular incentives for extra or exceptional work.

<u>Luxury gift certificates</u>.

Luxury certificates could include: a day at a spa, dinner for two at a four-star restaurant, beauty make-over from a renowned hairstylist and makeup artist, a bouquet of fresh flowers sent to the employee's spouse every month for a year, a free airplane flying lesson, tickets to the hottest show in town complete with limousine service to and from the theatre, weekend getaways, boat rentals, etc. Any number of these luxury certificates could become prize choices for employees.

<u>Debit accounts</u>.

Many incentive businesses offer catalogs that display merchandise available for a certain amount of points. Employees can accumulate points to save up and redeem for specific items from those catalogs. Or, in a less formal way, choose a variety of specific items of merchandise from a local store to offer as prizes redeemable for points 'on the spot.'

Summary

Once you've mastered the art of hiring and providing incentives, you will be rewarded with a stable and powerful workforce that puts 'superstars' on your team, and the power of productivity into your bottom line.

The following five creative motivators will help you to jump-start your own business tactics to keep those valuable employees. Use them to brainstorm your own programs to give your employees programs they will look forward to participating in.

Creative Motivator #1:

Host a
"Knowledge Is Profit"
Quiz Program

This incentive program is great for any business to encourage employees — new and current — to learn all they can about products, services and procedures.

The Program:

Design a customized game of "Jeopardy" in which ALL employees can participate. This program works best for small businesses (less than 15 employees) or individual departments of a larger company. This is especially beneficial to companies that either have a high turnover rate or a constant stream of new hires due to growth.

The Set-up:

Depending on the number of employees in your business, 'contestants' can either be individuals or placed into teams. For instance, if you have three employees, then each of the three should play individually. If you have four employees, you could have four individual players or two teams of two. If you have five employees, three could be the 'players' and two could be the 'question makers'. The players get the points if they answer correctly. The question makers get the points if the player answers incorrectly.

The business owner, manager or supervisor acts as the moderator.

Predetermine several categories for your Jeopardy board. From 4 to 8 categories would be ideal. For example, if you owned a pet supply shop, you might label categories as:

- Name that Kibble (questions about pet food ingredients and nutrition comparisons)

- Fowl Language (questions about birds)

- Sit Up & Roll Over (questions about pet training and toys) and

- Habitat Schmabitat (questions about cages, modular structures/ pet furniture, and carriers)

Unless you have had to divide participants into players and question makers, ask ALL employees to submit at least 20-40 questions and answers, five for each of the 4-8 predetermined categories. Questions and answers are to be given to the moderator(s) a day prior to 'show time', separated into the appropriate categories and written individually on 3 x 5 index cards. The moderator reviews the submissions, eliminates duplicates, and places the remaining cards into shoeboxes; use a separate box for each category.

On a monthly, bimonthly or quarterly basis, schedule a day to play the Jeopardy game. The owner pays to have pizza or sandwiches and soft drinks delivered after hours. Use an inexpensive kitchen timer to set the allotted amount of playing time (10-15 minutes is sufficient) for each round. Using a bulletin board, chalk board, white board or writing easel, post the category titles in a horizontal row across the top.

How to Play

While you can certainly play the game with one round of 15 minutes, consider two rounds of 10-15 minutes each. Since there is no specific degree of difficulty for each question, all points are the same for each question.

The moderator shuffles the contents of each shoebox (category). When a subject is chosen, the moderator chooses a card at random from that category box.

Players take turns choosing the subject category. Each contestant (or team of contestants) writes down the answer to each question. A time limit should be imposed for completion of the answer as well. Perhaps 10 or 15 seconds per answer.

Once a question is asked, the moderator turns that card face down in front of him/her. Once an answer is written, the contestant turns that card face down in front of him/her. Each subsequent question and answer is placed faced down directly on top of the previous question/answer.

At the end of the round, the moderator turns his/her stack of cards face up and rereads the first question. Each contestant turns his/her stack of cards face up and each reads their answer. The moderator then verifies correct answers and assigns points. <u>ALL contestants with the right answer receive the points</u>. The purpose of this game is not to determine who is the quickest with an answer. The purpose of this game is to encourage all employees to learn the answers.

Business Benefit

The more employees know and remember about your products, services and procedures, the more likely they will apply the knowledge when working with your customers and performing internal tasks and procedures. Making a contest out of having the knowledge will result in a conscious effort on the part of employees to remember and use the things they are taught.

BONUS BENEFIT: While contestants will put some effort into studying for the game, they will also derive benefits from the process of being responsible for creating the questions.

Creative Motivator #2:

Catch Employees
Doing Things Right!

The concept of a Secret Shopper program is not new. Briefly, businesses hire organizations that will send out people to either shop a store or make inquiries at a business to 'test' how employees respond to customers when the owner is not around.

These organizations then report back the detailed results to the business owner. From the receptionist position and on through managerial staff, a business owner can receive feedback with a customer perspective.

While these 'secret shopper' programs are often detested by employees because they feel they are being mistrusted and spied on, adding a new twist to the process can turn it into an incentive-based program.

Here's the twist:

1. Use the secret shopper method to catch employees doing things RIGHT!
2. Reward the employee on the spot!

Why this incentive program works:

Employees respond more to recognition of what they do right than they do to reprimand for the things they do wrong. By rewarding the things they are doing right, you pave the way for the employee to want to do MORE things right.

When choosing this incentive program, keep the following in mind:

Inform employees. Let employees know that you have implemented this program. Tell them that at any time someone posing as a customer may be the secret shopper. Also tell them that any employee who gives this 'secret shopper' exceptional service will be rewarded on the spot with certificates for either cash or prizes. If you are trying to train employees to say or do specific things as outlined in your procedures, let them know that the secret shopper will be looking for those exact things.

By telling employees what the shopper will be looking for, you increase the chances that each employee will be conscientious about learning that specific procedure. Once learned (even when the incentive is no longer for that criteria), there is a good chance that the employee will continue to do things correctly.

Provide specific criteria to the agency for each month's shopping trip.

When you hire the secret shopper service, be sure to provide very specific criteria for reward presentation. Performance must be based not only on the customer getting what he/she wants, but getting it in the way you have outlined the procedure.

For instance, you may be trying to train the receptionist to answer the phone or greet a visitor using a certain phrase (or variation of a phrase). The receptionist may be pleasant and helpful, but if she does not use that specific phrase, no reward will be presented.

Stagger the 'secret shopper' schedule.

Don't hire a company to send someone out once each month or once per week. Employees will soon figure out that if the shopper appears on a Monday, there won't be another one for at least a week (or month). Have someone come two days in a row, or even two times in one day! It may even be in your best interest to not know the schedule yourself. Explain that you want a secret shopper to visit 10 times (or however often you want) in a 30-day period. Give the company certificate vouchers to hand employees. Employees present the vouchers to you to redeem the prizes.

Vary the rewards.

Vary the value of rewards so employees never know if they'll be handed a coupon for a free lunch, a $10 bill, a night on the town, or a trip for two to Las Vegas. While there may be more lunches and $10 bills handed out than trips, if employees know that the value could be high, the incentive will be stronger to maintain peak performance each and every day with each and every customer.

Include all job positions.

Every position in the company is important to the business you gain, keep or lose. Make sure that it is just as possible for a receptionist to win rewards as it is for a salesperson to win them.

The Benefit

You get employees who are eager to do their jobs well each and every day.

Creative Motivator #3:

Team Goal Getters!

Rewards based on individual performance are great motivators. Yet, team programs give employees a reason to look at coworkers as comrades instead of competitors. If you have a two or three person office, the entire office can be working together to reach a specific goal. Otherwise teams of two, three, four or more can be put into competition against each other.

Programs conducive to team incentives include:

Membership drives.
Health clubs, associations, private golf or tennis clubs, or any business that rewards customers with 'membership' in specific benefit programs can give employees an opportunity to compete in teams.

How to organize the drive:

Be sure to designate a start date and a finish date for the program. Clearly state (and document) the rules. For instance, the rewards will be based on new memberships only, not current members who renew. If different membership levels are available, then the points system should be based on a dollar amount or membership level, not just the number of new members signed up. For instance, if you have three levels of membership available, employee teams would score 1 point for the lowest cost level, 2 points for the middle level, and 3 points for the highest cost level of membership.

It is usually beneficial to offer a number of smaller rewards along the way so that one team doesn't so far exceed the others that the others stop trying. For instance, the ultimate goal may be that whatever team reaches the highest points scored by the deadline date, wins whatever the BIG prize is. But, along the way, set up milestones that other teams can win just by reaching that milestone.

For instance, any team that signs up 5 new members gets to go out to lunch on the company to strategize their next move. Any team that signs up another 5 (for a total of 10) new members is given a half day off (with pay) for each member. The ultimate prize could be 3-day weekends for a month for each team member, a team trip to an afternoon ballgame paid for by the company, etc. Base prizes based on the income you stand to gain with new memberships. Employees know if they are being rewarded fairly.

Have each team give themselves a team name.

Use brightly colored charts or toy race tracks (with one race car tagged with each team name) to mark goal milestones.

Set a time limit, and a final reward for the winning team. On the final day of the membership drive, award prizes and celebrate. Acknowledge that everyone did a great job and surprise the entire staff by ordering pizza to be delivered at closing, or have specialty items inscribed like coffee mugs that said, "I survived the membership drive of '99". Better yet, do both!

<u>Better Business Solution Teams</u>.
Many solutions to corporate problems can be solved by going to the people who work the floor every day. Increased productivity, overhead reduction, quality improvement and overall efficiency are constant issues that management deals with. By sharing your business goals with employees, and giving them an opportunity to help solve them, you can improve profits – and employee morale – by soliciting their participation.

How to organize the program:

Determine several "Team Challenges" based on corporate goals.

• Set the criteria for each Team Challenge
For instance, you may want to suggest that a team have at least three members. Or, if this is a large company, you may want to suggest that a team have 3-5 members representing different departments. Or, you may decide a problem should be solved by a team made up of different positions in the company (i.e., a manager, a sales person, and someone from the accounting department).

• Decide on a reward for each Team Challenge

Rewards should be individualized to the degree of difficulty (or benefit to the company). Rewards are not guaranteed for submitting the proposal. Like any other incentive program, not everyone wins. Rewards are given only if the plan — or a revised version of the plan — is implemented. If a proposal looks promising, but needs more work, go back to the team and explain what 'works' and what doesn't. Give them an opportunity to improve upon it. If you implement the plan, involve the team members.

• Make an announcement

Announce to all employees that a Solution Teams incentive program is being implemented.

• Post the Team Challenges

Post the team challenges on a bulletin board or white board; Let them know where to find the opportunities.

When a Team successfully completes and submits a winning solution, make a big deal out of it. Announce it in a meeting or circulate a memo. Remind others of the rewards that were presented. Have plaques made up that say, "Team Challenge Winner for <name of the challenge> and inscribe that person's name on it.

Team Challenge ideas may include:

Give Yourself a Raise Challenge, in which a team can prepare a plan to reduce overhead by 20%. If the plan is successfully implemented, each member of the team will get a raise (either a percentage or dollar figure increase);

Efficiency Challenge, in which a team devises a plan to expedite customer orders, deliveries or internal communications — without increasing costs. Each team member could receive 3-day weekends (with pay) for a month.

Customer Satisfaction Challenge, in which a team devises a customer satisfaction survey and implementation process. You determine the things you want to know from your customers. Team members are rewarded based on how many surveys are returned by customers.

Incentive Challenge, in which employees come up with ideas for your next incentive program that is beneficial to the company and the employee.

Trash Challenge. Getting employees to recycle (paper, pop cans, plastic, glass, etc.) is often a big problem. The bigger the company, the bigger the problem. Let an employee solutions team tackle the problem and devise a plan that makes it easy for employees to recycle. The reward for team members might be a cut of the savings (or profits) that the company is reimbursed for recycling.

Creative Motivator #4:

Charity Drives!

It may be surprising to know that many employees are motivated by being able to serve their favorite charities with the support of employers. While this motivator may not directly affect your bottom line profits, the exposure in the community as a charity-conscious company will reap benefits of recognition and potential business.

Many organizations donate money, participate in food drives or provide incentives for employee contributions to the United Way, but employees who are allowed to get involved (especially on company time), reap great satisfaction and uplifted morale.

Here are a few ideas to get the charitable wheels turning:

- Give employees paid time off to help with community charities. For instance, a local food drive may need people to help collect donations, load trucks or separate donated items. Let employees know they can use up to 5 hours per week (paid) to donate their hands-on help for the duration of the drive. They may also be considered for additional requested time off (unpaid).

- Donate employee volunteer manpower for a local Habitat for Humanity house building project. Find out what the project needs are, post the needs for employees to view, and then decide on how much time off you can afford to donate for the project.

- Encourage employees to participate on charitable committees. Allow time for them to attend meetings on company time. Be receptive to requests they make for additional support (either monetary or manpower).

- Involve employees in determining where your company donation dollars are distributed. Ask employees to recommend local charities they think deserve help and explain why the company should support this particular cause. Present the recommended charities to all employees in ballot form and have them 'elect' the charity they'd like to see the company support. Once elected, ask employees for ideas on how best to support the chosen charity. Some ideas include:

Retailers can donate a percentage of annual profits.

Companies can sponsor a specific event (bake sale, bazaar, auction, etc.) to raise money for this specific charity.

Employees donate one hour's pay per week for a specific length of time.

Each employee can volunteer one day per month (paid) to help with whatever the charity needs.

Creative Motivator #5:

Sweat the Small Stuff Competition!

Here is another creative motivator with a team concept in mind. Do you have a Suggestion Box? If not, why not? And, if so, are you (the owner or management personnel) the only one responding to suggestions, complaints, and problems? There's a better way! Employees are a great resource for viewing the business from the ground floor — both for recognizing the problems *and* the solutions. Employee team efforts to devise solutions to the day-to-day problems will benefit you as a company and give employees the power to affect change — and be rewarded for those efforts.

How to organize the plan:

In a large company, teams can be made up of volunteers who sign up for participation. In a small company, I encourage you to ask everyone to participate since they all work so closely together.

Teams should consist of 5 members per team. In small companies, it can be as few as 3 members per team, or if the staff employee count is less than 5, then all 5 can work together. The point is to give teams a diverse perspective so there is enough 'brainstorming power' to discuss possibilities and find viable solutions.

Determine rewards. Perhaps use a simple reward system that each solution implemented has a reward of time off for each team member, merchandise from the store, free passes to movies, etc. Make it worth the team's time to put effort into the project. And if two or more teams come up with similar solutions to a problem, award all team members. To keep teams in competition with each other, at the end of the year (or quarter, or whatever time length you choose), the team that submits the MOST implemented suggestions, receives an extra reward. In the case of a tie, the tie will be broken and only one team wins.

On a regular basis (monthly, quarterly, etc.) the suggestion box should be emptied. Review suggestions for duplication or for those that do not require a response.

Remaining 'active' suggestions are to be typed onto a sheet of paper and distributed to all teams, along with any 'rules' and the deadline for submission.

Teams are to meet on their own time (before work, during lunch breaks, after work) to work on the problems. For each problem that they can not find a solution for, require a statement of reasons why it was difficult for the problem to be solved (this could lead to acquiring additional information that may eventually lead to a solution).

Determine a specific date when solutions are to be presented. This can be done in a full group forum, or, if there are many teams, a team captain can be appointed to present the information. Presentation should be done face to face with the owner or manager so that any questions can be immediately answered.

Implement good ideas! Reward the employees for a job well done.

Any of the problems that were unsolvable by any of the teams could be used as extra credit (or extra points) projects. If it is a problem worth finding a solution for, encourage employees to think harder and smarter by sweetening the reward pot!

BONUS Creative Motivator:

Liberally Dole Out
Pats on Their Backs!

Don't ignore the little things that acknowledges your appreciation of an employee's worth:

- Say "thank you for doing such a great job on _____" (fill in the blank with the specific task).

- Have "Thanks for going above and beyond the call of duty!" business sized cards printed. Hand them out to anyone who expends extra effort or completes a task by putting in extra time. Employees who collect 10 cards can trade them in for a free lunch or some other small token of thanks.

- Give credit where credit is due. NEVER take credit for something that an employee has done. ALWAYS recognize that person's contribution in front of his/her peers and superiors.

- Once a month have an employee of the day voted for by other employees. On that day, the boss (or supervisor/manager) has to do that employee's least favorite task.

- The business owner hosts a holiday hors d'oeuvre or dinner party for employees who have received at least one recognition reward for the year.

- Every new employee is to spend an hour prior to, and then be treated to lunch by the boss. The business owner gets a chance to talk about the business philosophy and know the employee on a personal basis. The employee can ask questions that can't be answered by a manager or other employee. By having the boss take the time to spend with a new employee, the employee feels more important to the business.

In Conclusion:

Whatever you use to motivate your employees, remember these key ingredients for success:

- Actively promote the program
- Clearly state its purpose
- Set challenging but achievable goals
- Place a time limit on results
- Keep rules uncomplicated
- Make sure rewards coincide with employee desires!

Addendum II

Financial Aid Resource Guide

Raising capital to start or fund a business can be a frustrating process. Some of us don't even know where to begin to search for information on how to determine how much we need. Others of us have reached a plateau and want to start searching for financing to take us to the next level of growth.

Whether you are just starting out and need to learn the basics, or you've been in business for awhile and need expansion or growth financing, the following financial resources guide is designed to point you in the right direction.

There are literally thousands of resources to turn to for information on specific funding. It would be impossible to list them all here since they change by state and new sources are introduced every year. What we have listed in this Addendum is:

1. Cash flow strategies that may help deter the need for financial assistance.
2. A glossary of financing venues to help you decide which types of financing programs fit your specific needs.
3. Recommendations on how to conduct your research.
4. How to increase your chances of getting the cash you need.

5. A resources list for finding information and funding sources and agencies.

Cash Flow Strategies:

<u>Business Incubators</u>

Business incubators are designed to encourage entrepreneurship. They are usually comprised of organizing a facility to house a number of small or growing companies and enterprises to share services such as secretarial, accounting, meeting rooms, etc. The objective is to reduce some of the overhead costs associated with a single-company facility and free up cash flow.

<u>Credit Card Advances</u>

Borrowing from your credit cards is technically a financing option since you incur debt and pay interest on your advance 'loan' amount. However, because the tactic provides immediate access to funds and there is no prequalification or application process, we are including this option as part of the cash flow strategy list. Remember that this is a loan like any other and failure to pay off the debt will result in bigger problems later on.

<u>Customer Prepay</u>

Offering discounts to customer who prepay can significantly increase your cash flow. The cost of carrying unpaid accounts receivable can be far more expensive than discounting for payment up front.

<u>Inventory Clearance Sales</u>

If you have aging inventory taking up space in your warehouse, clear it out! Off-season sales and first-come, first-served clearance sales are a good way to raise quick cash.

Rental Arrangements

Do you have office or warehouse/storage space that you could section off and rent on a month-to-month, cash up front basis? Depending on your business type, you may also find it beneficial to make some of your products available on a short-term rental basis.

Trade and Barter

A practice that has successfully existed for decade upon decade is a trade and barter arrangement. Whenever possible, strike up mutually beneficial trade agreements. Small businesses are prime candidates for this type of product/service swap. For instance, an accountant may need computer help, and a computer consultant may need accounting services. Decide on what an even trade would be for services and take advantage of the opportunity. By not having to use cash funds to pay out for the services or products you need, you are able to free up cash that can be better used for other parts of the business.

Vendor or Supplier Relationships

If you have been a good, loyal customer to your vendors and suppliers, these relationships can prove invaluable when you are in a short-term cash-crunch. Companies that stand to benefit from your success are often willing to make special arrangements. For instance: ask for extended credit for a specific length of time. If you are normally expected to pay within 30 days, ask for 45, 60 or 90-day extensions; renegotiate equipment lease payments; or, ask for inventory on a consignment basis. Be sure that whatever promises you make to your vendors for these leniencies, you keep. You need to maintain the trust you've already built with these suppliers.

Glossary of Financing Venues:

Conventional Loans

Bank lending for small and growing companies appears to parallel the health of the economy. When interest rates are low, banks are more prone to rolling out the red carpet to small businesses. Finding conventional financing has traditionally been a matter of opportunity afforded by current economic conditions. However in the past few years, many banks have been promoting themselves as 'your small business partner' and have begun to acknowledge the revitalized growth of entrepreneurial businesses. When looking for conventional funding, contact several banks. Each has its own set of specific criteria for loan approvals and can tell you exactly what they'll be looking for when they review your application. Listen to them carefully and ask questions if you don't understand. *Short-term loans* are also an option depending on your specific need for a loan. Explore this option for purposes such as financing accounts receivable for a short length of time (30-90 days), or to build a seasonal inventory over a 4-5 month period of time. Banks grant short term loans based on your general credit reputation and can be either an unsecured loan, or a secured loan.

Corporate Angels

Corporate Angels are a diverse population of individuals who provide seed capital for inventors and start-up firms, and equity financing for established small firms. Good candidates for corporate angel funding are entrepreneurs trying to raise $100,000 to $1,000,000 for ventures that are unlikely to be publicly held or acquired by a larger firm within a five to ten year time period. Thus, they do not attract venture capital investors. According to the Office of Small Business Research and Development of the National Science Foundation, angels tend to invest close to home. They like to stay in touch with ventures they finance, often providing invaluable guidance.

Factoring (Accounts Receivable) Financing

Factoring is a term used to borrow against your expected income (accounts receivable) for immediate cash. With hefty interest rates, this can be a costly means to raise capital. Thoroughly investigate all of your options before choosing this type of financing.

Government Grants

Both state and federal government grants are available to small business owners. If you can get them, they're a great way to start or grow your business. Grants are *free* money, not a loan, so you do not have the added pressure of having to pay the money back. Each grant has its own specific criteria for qualification and grants have a varied range of funding amounts available, depending on the budgeted total allotment of the grant program. Grants are available for specific industries, minorities, teenagers, and inventions and research projects. This is a great resource with which to start your search.

Issuing Stock

If you have incorporated your business, your charter specifies the amount of shares the corporation is authorized to issue. You may be able to raise equity funds by selling shares of stock, making those who purchase them part owners of your business.

Joint Ventures

A joint venture is a business arrangement in which two or more parties undertake a specific economic activity together. They are popular with businesses interested in expansion and can help with cost-effectively uncovering new markets, and create a new profit center.

Private Investors

Private investors can be family members, friends, business associates, etc. This is primarily any loan or financial assistance received from individuals and not governed by state of federal regulation.

Purchase Order Financing

Similar to Factoring, you can acquire interim financing based on orders you have received from creditworthy customers.

SBA Loans

The Small Business Administration (SBA) has helped thousands of small companies through multiple loan programs to help them get started, expand and prosper. By law, before you can use SBA assistance, an applicant must first seek financing from a bank or other lending institution. Most banks offer SBA loan assistance when the bank itself cannot provide funding. SBA offers two basic types of business loans: guarantee loans and direct loans.

Guarantee loans are made by private lenders, usually banks, and guaranteed up to 90% by SBA. The maximum guarantee percentage of loans exceeding $155,000 is 85%. SBA can guarantee up to $750,000 of a private sector loan.

Direct loans have an administrative maximum of $150,000 and are available only to applicants unable to secure an SBA-guaranteed loan.

SBICs and MESBICs

Small Business Investment Corporations (SBICs) are licensed to provide financial services to small business in the form of equity/

venture financing for modernization, expansion, etc. The SBIC usually seeks to purchase stock in the company and become involved in actual business operations by providing management direction. Minority Enterprise Small Business Investment Corporations (MESBICs) provide identical financial support to small enterprises that are minority-owned.

State and Local Funding

State and local financial programs are an excellent resource for small business funding. States and individual communities take an active interest in maintaining a healthy economy through business development. In addition to loan programs, numerous other programs may be of interest to you such as network and support programs, export assistance, and state contracts. For information, contact your local chamber of commerce.

Venture Capital

While it is not impossible for new companies to receive venture capital funding, it is unlikely. Venture capital supports firms that exhibit above-average growth rates, a significant potential for market expansion, and are in need of additional financing to sustain growth or further research and development. Sources of venture capital financing include public and private pension funds, commercial banks and bank holding companies, Small Business Investment Companies licensed by the SBA, private venture capital firms, insurance companies, investment management companies, bank trust departments, industrial companies seeking to diversify their investments, and investment bankers acting as intermediaries for themselves or other investors.

Venture Capital Limited Partnerships: Investors' money is pooled and invested in money market assets until venture investments — primarily for young, technology-oriented businesses — are selected.

The general partners are experienced investment managers who select and invest the equity and debt securities of firms with high growth potential and the ability to go public in the near future. Other

Other creative ways to finance your business by relying on your own assets include:

Take out a loan on your savings passbook. The bank will charge you interest, but the funds you maintain on deposit in your account continue to earn interest, which reduces the overall interest rate on the loan.

Take out a new or refinance an existing mortgage. If you own your own home or other real property, you are able to refinance the mortgage you owe on, or mortgage property that is already paid. Balance current mortgage rates against your rate of return to ensure this option is viable.

Take out a loan against your life insurance policy. If you have a life insurance policy that has accumulated cash value over the years, this could be a viable option. Loans on such policies generally have a low interest rate.

How to Conduct Your Research

1. **The Internet**. In all aspects of research that I perform as a writer and small business owner, I believe that the Internet is one of the best research tools around — and the fastest way to find information. If you aren't computer-literate or have no desire to learn how to navigate the 'information superhighway' I urge you to reconsider. However if you absolutely refuse to use the technology, it might be worth the money spent to assign your financial research to an independent contractor (or

computer-savvy student) who does know how to use the Internet. Information published in books and reports can become quickly outdated; information on the Internet is updated in real time. If at all possible, use the Internet's capabilities to begin your research. You'll see many of the resources in this Addendum point to useful web sites for both start-ups and expansion business financing.

2. **Your Local Library**. Do-it-yourselfers (like myself) can usually be found browsing the stacks at the local library. I find as much information as possible via the Internet and, based on the results, follow up that research with a trip to the library. There are many resources, including videos, directories and books written on the subject of financing. While this resource list refers to many of the ones I've found to be valuable, there are always more to find lurking on the library shelves. Librarians are wonderful partners in tracking down resource material.

3. **Find a Mentor**. Friends or associates who have already experienced the frustrating process of finding new funding can be great sources of information. They are often just as willing to share mistakes they made as well as the successes accomplished. Having someone who can answer your immediate questions can expedite your process.

4. **Hire an Advisor**. While many of us are reluctant to hire a consultant to help us, most times the money is well spent. Take into consideration the time you have to devote to the research. Weigh it against the cost of the time you spend away from your business to do so. Interview several advisors to determine exactly what you can expect for the money you spend. Then decide how much you want to 'go it alone' or how cost-effective hiring a consultant might be.

Increase Your Chances for Getting the Cash You Need

There is no quick and easy way to get your hands on the cash you need for start-up or expansion. It takes hard work, realistic goals and the ability to present your proposal with confidence, including facts and figures to back up your claim to your business' potential success.

The more you can anticipate what lenders look for in your proposal, the better prepared you will be to give it to them. You have a very short amount of time to catch the interest of lenders and investors. Don't ruin your chances with a dynamite concept and lousy presentation.

The following suggestions for increasing your odds for getting the cash you need come from a variety of lending professionals who evaluate proposals and make lending decisions every day:

- <u>Enthusiasm for your business is good; facts and figures are better.</u> Too many entrepreneurs try to convince potential lenders to "buy into" the concept of their business while trying to forego the evidence of its viability. You need to sell your lender on the future cash-generating capabilities of the business.

- <u>Ask potential financiers what they need from you.</u> Requirements of a bank may be far different from that of a private investor or venture capitalist. The goal is to eliminate assumptions on both of your parts.

- <u>If possible, meet the person handling your request before submitting an application or proposal.</u> Better yet, invite the potential lender to your place of business and do a well-planned show and tell of your current status, and future possibilities.

- <u>Turn your business plan into a business loan package</u>. Include significant data about past, current and future performance.

- <u>It's a common mistake for small business owners to use past tax returns as the sole evidence that they can handle the requested debt</u>. While it is true that you will probably be asked to submit them, don't stop there! Concentrate on credible financial projections for the term of the loan request.

- <u>Don't 'shotgun' your loan request to many lenders</u>. Tailor it to the specific lender most likely to grant your request. When possible, cultivate the relationship before requesting a loan.

- <u>Motivate the loan officer to pick your presentation out of the many on his/her desk by using a well-thought out cover letter, photographs and summary of salient facts</u>. You can use graphics if they add to your presentation, but use them sparingly so they do not distract from the information or make your presentation look amateurish.

- <u>Be knowledgeable about the process of raising capital</u>. Get advice or seek a mentor to help you understand the process.

Let the Research Begin!

Here are resources to help you get started in your travels through the financing maze.

Books:

If you browse the bookshelves of your local library or bookstores, you will find so many resources on small business development it will make your head spin! Here are some of the books currently available that are very specific to raising capital:

Borrowing for Your Business: Winning the Battle for the Banker's "Yes", George M. Dawson, published by Upstart, $19.95

Cash Flow Problem Solver: Common Problems and Practical Solutions, Bryan E. Milling, published by Sourcebooks Trade, $19.95

Cash In On Cash Flow: 50 Tough-as-Nails Ideas for Revitalizing Your Business, David Silver, published by AMACO (American Management Association), $24.95

Directory of Venture Capital, Catherine E. Lister & Thomas D. Harnish, published by John Wiley & Sons, $34.95

Financing Your Small Business: Techniques for Planning, Acquiring and Managing Debt, Arthur R. DeThomas, published by Oasis, $19.95

Finding Your Wings: How to Locate Private Investors to Fund Your Venture, Gerald A. Benjamin & Joel Margulis, published by John Wiley & Sons. $34.95

Free Money for Small Business and Entrepreneurs, Laurie Blum, published by John Wiley & Sons, $14.95

Government Giveaways for Entrepreneurs: Over 9,000 Sources of $$, Help & Information to Start or Expand Your Business, Matthew Lesko, published by Information USA Inc., $33.95

The Insider's Guide to Small Business Loans, Dan M. Koehler, published by Oasis, $19.95

Money Sources for Small Business: How to Find Private, State, Federal, and Corporate Financing, William Alarid, published by Puma Publishing Company, $19.95

Pratt's Guide to Venture Capital Sources, edited by Daniel Bokser, published by Securities Data Publishing, $355

Raising Capital: The Grant Thornton LLP Guide for Entrepreneurs, Michael C. Bernstein and Lester Wolosoff, published by Irwin, $50.00

The Small Business Financial Resource Guide. **FREE** 151-page paperback compiled by Braddock Communications. Write: U.S. Chamber of Commerce Small Business Center, 1615 H St. NW, Washington, DC 20062.

The Small Business Insider's Guide to Bankers, Suzanne Caplan & Thomas M. Nunnally, published by Oasis Press, $18.95

Internet resources for funding information:

Visit this site for an explanation of the ins and outs of receivables financing options.

www.gotmoney.com/serv02.htm

This is America's Business Funding Directory loan finder. It is a free, fill-in-the-blank service to match users to potential lenders.

www.businessfinance.com

This site is the online companion to MoneyHunt TV to entertain, educate and empower entrepreneurs who seek capital to start, buy or grow a business. Includes a business plan template and the Golden Rolodex to locate sources on the web that track investors.

www.moneyhunter.com

This is the Small Business Administration's online information site. The site has a list of federally licensed Small Business Investment Companies including names, contacts, and the type of loans each prefers to make.

www.sbaonline.sba.gov

American Express provides a wealth of information for the small business owner. You'll find some good information here regarding financing options.

www.americanexpress.com/smallbusiness/resources/

This site has compiled a comprehensive list of banks.

www.qualisteam.com/eng/confusa.html

These two sites give general and detailed lists of venture-capital firms.

www.findingmoney.com/body.html
www.vfinance.com/ventcap.htm

Business Week magazine hosts an information-intensive web site. The online version is a great resource to search the articles archives to find financing information and advice.

www.businessweek.com/smallbiz

Inc. magazine online has a searchable business funding database to help small business connect with funding opportunities.

www.inc.com

Learn about investing criteria of Small Business Investment Companies (SBICs), and read about companies that have succeeded under SBIC instruction.

www.hostlink.com/nasbic/index.html

Here's a great site for advice and general information about financing, terminology, and definitions.

www.capital-connection.com

If you are interested in leasing as an option to alleviate cash flow problems, this site has a glossary of typical terms used in leasing deals.

www.bworks.com/funding

These two sites have sample business plans for a variety of different company types.

www.bplans.com/sample.htm

www.once.com/gcg

Magazines:

Magazines that cater to small businesses are a great resource of information. Many have recurring columns specifically written about financial challenges and funding options.

Search the library for back issues of any of the following magazines to find pertinent information on small business financing:

Business Start-Ups
Entrepreneur Magazine
Inc. & Inc. Technology
Independent Business
Opportunity Magazine
Self-Employed Professional
Success Magazine

Organizations:

State and local organizations can be a wealth of information to you. Information about state grants and funding, local education and partnership initiatives, and business incubators can be acquired by contacting your local area chamber of commerce or your state Department of Economic Trade and Development.

Note: Resources listed here are intended for research purposes only. This information is not intended to endorse any specific program or agency.

About the Author

Susan Carter is a freelance writer, editor and small business consultant. Her expertise in strategic plan development to fit small business budgets led her to form Nasus Publishing, a company dedicated to developing informational materials and resources of success-building ideas for best use of your time and money. You can reach Susan via the internet at:

susancarter@successideas.com

Also by Susan Carter:

SPLASH Marketing for Overworked Small Business Owners

Download 3 Free Chapters at
http://www.successideas.com

29 Ways To Increase Profits and Productivity

This 70+ page ebook is **FREE** when you subscribe to Carter's (free) monthly ezine, SuccessExpress Press! Quick and easy sign-up.

Business-Building E-Classes

Get one-on-one, business-building consultation from Susan Carter. This virtual format allows you to get start-to-finish, step-by-step instruction, and direct feedback and recommendations that address your specific business challenges. With my e-classes you can:

√ Work at your own pace,
√ Accommodate your personal schedule, and
√ Save thousands in consulting fees typcially associated with traditional on-site service.

To learn more about the above books and e-classes, visit:
http://www.successideas.com

Sign up for our FREE monthly e-zine, SuccessExpress Press!